$28

2857

Politics in Czechoslovakia, 1945–1990

by
John F.N. Bradley

EAST EUROPEAN MONOGRAPHS, BOULDER
DISTRIBUTED BY COLUMBIA UNIVERSITY PRESS, NEW YORK

1991

EAST EUROPEAN MONOGRAPHS, NO. CCCXV

CONTENTS

PREFACE

This book was sponsored by the British Social Sciences Research Council in 1968, under the impact of the reforms in Czechoslovakia. I was then member of the Government Department at the University of Manchester and the research was going to be put to use in the new courses on the communist system in Eastern Europe. For a time I used the accumulated research materials for lectures, which in the case of Czechoslovakia were concerned with a historical survey and institutional analyses.

Only in 1980 was the book ready for publication. The lectures were put into book form, but since no changes appeared in the re-established totalitarian system, the research findings were left uncorrected. Ten years later, after the 'velvet' revolution certain chapters had to be completed or modified, but no largescale corrections were necessary. All was simply put into the past tense and the Czechoslovak totalitarian system became the subject of study for political scientists and their students as a historical subject, which gave me immense pleasure.

Henceforth Western students can study totalitarianism in the Czechoslovak form either as contemporary history or as a political science subject without developmental aspect. Since Czechoslovakia had been democratic before communism, the book can be used as a demonstration of the devastating effect communism had on freedom, human rights and liberal democracy in general. This was the main reason, why it was thought pertinent to republish the title, now almost unobtainable. In contrast to the original publication footnotes etc. were left out as unnecessary. Instead a detailed bibliography was added. As for the 'Velvet Revolution' which gently abolished this violent system, it is the subject of my next book. This volume demonstrates the weaknesses of the supposedly omnipotent totalitarian system, which it brought down so easily.

May I put on record my thanks to all my Czech and Slovak friends, who helped me with the writing of it, either by providing documentary evidence or invaluable advice. I was unable to list them in the previous edition and it gives me great pleasure to do so now: Dr. J. Křížek, Dr. Navrátil, Dr. Z. Šolle, Dr. Prečan, J. Umlauf, the late J. Sadovský, Dr. Pichlík, the late Academician Holotík, Dr. Plevza, Dr. Ján Mlynárik, Dr. Musil, Dr. Jiří Kolař, Dr. Vrána and many others. Special thanks go to the late Sir Cecil Parott, who purchased some research materials for the University of Lancaster and helped with critical commentary. My American colleagues, Professors Stephen Fischer-Galati, Josef Kalvoda and Joe Zacek, have my gratitude for their kindness in helping me with the publication. As all my publications were a family enterprise I must also thank my wife, my daughter Catherine, but above all my sons, Nicholas and Christopher, who undertook several dangerous research missions to Czechoslovakia on my behalf. I was unable to go there myself being under a 10-year sentence for espionage. It was while in prison that I in fact started this study of totalitarianism in the field.

John F.N. Bradley
Paris 1991

PART 1

INTRODUCTION

In 1945 Czechoslovakia emerged from the war more politically confused and disorganised than devastated. During the war in Bohemia some 3,014 buildings were destroyed and about 10,000 damaged. While material losses were heavier in Moravia (some 11,862 buildings destroyed and 19,000 damaged) Slovakia suffered damage only in 1944, after the Slovak uprising, when some sixty villages were burnt and destroyed by the German troops. In addition Slovakia was heavily damaged during the fighting between the Wehrmacht and the Red Army, but this destruction came to an end within six months. In any case, compared to the devastation of Germany, Czechoslovakia's was only minor.

What caused disorganization were the heavy casualties inflicted on the Czechs and Slovaks in a highly selective way by the Germans. Overall losses were relatively small: between September 1939 and May 1945 Czechoslovakia lost from 245,000 to 250,000 men, women and children. The war left behind between 100,000 and 127,816 cripples. Seventy-five thousand were executed and the Communist Party of Czechoslovakia alone lost 24,920 members, of whom 3,649 were executed and 5,687 died in concentration camps. However, what was most important about these losses was that they affected the intelligentsia, traditionally a group of people in charge of the political system and the economy of Czechoslovakia. Moreover, great population changes and movements increased the confusion and disorganisation of the leaderless people. Only in 1942 some 75,000 specialised workers were transported to Germany as forced labor; in 1943–4, some 32,000 more followed them and countless other workers were herded to Austria to build fortifications against the advancing Red Army. Economically the Germans disorganised Czechoslovakia as best they could; some 500,000 hectares of agricultural land were confiscated, Czech farmers driven away and the land was resettled with German

3

farmers. All these forcible displacements of population practically emptied the countryside and overcrowded the towns, where war industries clamoured for labour to replace the workers transported to Germany.

It was even more unfortunate that most of the casulaties and damage occurred during the last months of the war and that the casualties were the result of atrocities. In these few months the Czech provinces alone lost 52 per cent of locomotives and 68.3 per cent of its rolling stock: freight waggons suffered particularly bad damage (74.5 per cent were destroyed). In addition 63.5 per cent of lorries and 47.9 per cent of buses were ruined; 49 per cent of private cars disappeared and industrial production sank to 50 per cent of its pre-war capacity. During the last days of the war, during the uprising in Prague, 149 houses were destroyed and 633 more were heavily damaged: some 9,000 citizens died in the fighting. The whole republic was subjected to last minute atrocities usually committed by SS troops. In April 1945, Pleština was burnt down and twenty-eight inhabitants executed. Přerov, Rakovník and Nymburk were brutalised while thirty-four prisoners were executed at Trest. Fifty communist leaders who were rounded up in Prague were executed on 2 May 1945. These few examples are not exhaustive but show that, apart from bitterness and hatred, the German armies were leaving behind a leaderless population with its economic and political systems either destroyed or paralysed.

This was the situation on the spot, when President Beneš arrived in Prague from exile on 18 May 1945. He had been following the advance of the Red Army, taking over from it the liberated territories as soon as the Soviet armies moved on. His intentions were to re-establish the Czechoslovak republic and its political and constitutional system in the form it had assumed in pre-Munich days. Yet, during the war he had time to reflect, and now was determined to 'improve' the system, to correspond to the new conditions resulting from the war and its destruction.

In 1938 Dr Beneš was forced to abdicate as a result of the Munich agreement. But when during the war the Western allies declared the Munich agreement invalid, Beneš considered himself once again the constitutional head of Czechoslovakia. Now in May 1945, he was back in Czechoslovakia as President and, in the absence of an elected parliament, a virtual dictator. Because of the circumstances, he had to rule the country by means of decrees. But he decidedly wanted to restore liberal democracy, albeit modified, as soon as practicable. After years of dark fascist dictatorship, democracy in Czechoslovakia was going to be a presidential system, the President retaining most of the powers he had in the 1924 constitution. He was the titular head elected by parliament and responsible to it. However, he was also the Commander-in-Chief, had power of appointment over the executive, both the government and civil servants and in exceptional circumstances could act as dictator.

The President was prepared to share power with a parliament freely elected and with a government responsible to the latter. Political parties would participate in ruling the country through these two institutions and their share of power would be determined by the election results. This basic political framework was to be operated by professional civil servants and adjudicated by an independent judiciary. Furthermore, President Beneš envisaged several 'improvements': he was personally determined to become more of an arbiter than a chief executive, so far as the political situation would allow him. He was also determined to modify the party system, for their multiplicity had been a source of weakness in the first republic. The President therefore, proposed one party for each classical grouping, the left, centre and right. However, even before returning to Czechoslovakia, he was forced by the Czech Communists to change his intentions; their plan was for four parties to compete freely for power; the Communist Party and the Social Democratic on the left; the National Socialists (liberals) in the centre, and the People's Party (Catholic Party) on the right. In Slovakia the arrangement was even simpler. During the fighting in 1944–45 the Communist Party and the Democratic (liberal) Party were initially allowed to organise themselves. Two other parties were subsequently authorised, but never really got off the ground, and in the 1946 election proved an insignificant factor. The last modification to President Beneš's intentions seemed unimportant at the time, but proved immensely important in 1948: political parties were to be grouped in a coalition called the National Front and no one could share power, not even legally exist, except through this front. These were all negotiated concessions and modifications to President Beneš's schemes for post-war Czechoslovakia. However, developments on the spot brought further modifications.

Although President Beneš and his government had been recognized by all the Allies, including the USSR, it became clear (as in the case of Poland) that the President's and his government's real recognition would only come after Czechoslovakia's liberation. The problem was whether the USSR and the Red Army would allow President Beneš and his group to move back into Czechoslovakia and establish themselves there in power. The Red Army began to liberate Slovak territory late in 1944, and henceforth Czechoslovak territory was taken over by and administered by the Red Army and their natural allies, Czechoslovak Communists. In July 1944, when the Slovaks rose against the Germans, President Beneš saw this as a mixed blessing. He was overjoyed that the Slovaks had at long last acknowledged their past errors and guilt for the break-up of the Republic, but he also saw with dismay that the new political authority, the Slovak National Council, began to act without consulting him, sometimes even acting against his doctrines. Thus the risen Slovaks proclaimed themselves an independent nation equal to the Czechs, and the two Slovak political parties then in existence, the Slovak Communist Party and the Slovak Democratic Party, began to put into practice certain Communist ideas which the President had rejected as impracticable during negotiations with the Czechoslovak Communist leaders in Moscow in December 1943. Thus the Slovak National Council and its executives (commissioners) began to exercise powers of a national parliament and government, which was quite clearly contrary to President Beneš's post-war projects. Moreover, they began to exercise administrative powers in areas of the uprising and liberated regions through the ad hoc local and district councils (soviets) which the President opposed tooth and nail until December 1944, though he could do nothing about it. In addition the Slovaks put into practice another Communist idea, that of a political grouping or a sort of coalition called the National Front. This grouping, which would have far-reaching effect on the future political development of Czechoslovakia, determined local political arrangements allocating power more or less equally among the Slovak Communists, Democrats and non-party citizens.

Even as President Beneš and his entourage left London and arrived in Moscow, in December 1944, in order to move into the liberated parts of the country, they could not be sure of their fate. First of all they had to come to another agreement with the Czechoslovak Communist leaders, and only then move on. Great uncertainties lay ahead as President Beneš found out when he had sent his commissioners to the liberated Ruthenian territory. At first the Red Army let the commissioners in, but suddenly expelled them and abruptly annexed this formerly Czechoslovak region, known henceforth as Trans-Carpathian Ukraine. Thus, despite international recognition and agreements with the Communists, the London group and Beneš could be sure of nothing.

From the President's point of view the political process of liberation became alarming. As soon as the Red Army liberated a commune, town or city, it invariably dismissed the mayor, dissolved the council and appointed a national committee in their stead. Between 1944 and August 1945, some 4,855 such committees were appointed. The chairman was usually a local Communist, for the Red Army was aided in their choice of mayors by liaison officers from the Czechoslovak Army corps organised in the USSR, and these were invariably Communists. In Slovakia the representatives of the Slovak National Council, who were sometimes consulted by the Red Army, also tended to be Communist Party members and President Beneš had absolutely no control over this process. On 1 December, he had to put a brave face on it and legalise these ad hoc bodies by declaring them revolutionary local authorities. He only hoped that their political composition would be modified in the future after an election.

Without consulting the President, the Red Army proceeded a step further. Whenever it had liberated a district town it appointed the same ad hoc committees at this administrative level. In pre-war Czechoslovakia, district administration as professional and civil servants were appointed by the Ministry of the Interior. The Red Army claimed that the process was apparently a step towards a 'democratisation' of the Czechoslovak administration: the new district chairman had the same administrative powers as the old district chiefs, the hetmans (roughly comparable to French sous-prefets). Moreover, they were 'elected' by the new committees. The President was further disturbed to see that appointments to these district committees were not even based on pre-war election results. Thus at Michálovce, an Eastern Slovak district town, the district committee consisted of five workers, thirteen farmers, seven officials, three teachers, one tradesman, seven administrators, one housewife and three priests. More significantly, of these forty district councillors, seventeen were Communists and twenty-three non-party members. Thus, in practice, the agreement between Slovak Democrats and Communists on tripartite representation had not been observed. Though this sounded alarming, sometimes the explanation was simple: in the case of Michálovce, the Red Army declared that it could not appoint Slovak Democrats where there were none. It was a fact that non-Communist parties were thoroughly disorganised and the Communist Party was naturally taking advantage of it, wherever it could.

However, the Red Army could handle successfully even districts and cities where there were no Communists. Thus the Red Army liberated Brno, the Moravian capital, on 26 April 1945. The pre-war majority party, the National Socialists, headed an underground city council ready to take over the administration of the city. As soon as the Wehrmacht left the city, this council with an armed retinue arrived at the town hall, but were dissuaded from taking it over by the Red Army Major Kovtun and Czechoslovak Army Lieutenant Harus, the liaison officer and Communist leader. Next day, without any public announcement, an assembly 'elected' a thirty-member committee to run the city. Of these twelve were Communists, six Social Democrats, six National Socialists, four Christian Democrats (who were not present) and two non-party members. V. Matula, who was elected chairman (mayor), was a Communist Party member as well as his administrative officer, the secretary, F. Píšek. As a concession for this unfavourable division of power on the spot, the National Socialists were permitted to organise in Brno the Provincial Council of Moravia, administratively, though not politically, comparable to the Slovak National Council. Four political parties delegated their representatives to this paper council, whose chairman was elected F. Loubal, member of the National Socialist Party.

In Prague, the political situation was even more confused than in Brno. On 1 May 1945 Prague citizens became restless and panicky, and the following day they spontaneously rose against the German garrison. Only a few days before the uprising, the Gestapo arrested some fifty Communists and executed them. Still, on the day of the uprising, the vice-chairman of the Czech National Council, which took over the leadership of the revolt, was J. Smrkovský, a Communist leader. He entirely overshadowed the elderly Professor Pražák, who was its chairman. In the bloody confusion which followed, it seemed quite clear that neither the Czechs nor the Germans could win. The German army command happened to have near Prague the crack SS units (SS Panzer Division Wiking, SS Panzer Kampverband Wallenstein and units of the Army Corps commanded by General Reimann) and they instantly began to pound the city with their guns. The risen citizens erected some 16,000 barricades to oppose the Wehrmacht, but were on the point of surrender, when the tanks of Generals Rybalko and Lelyushenko reached Prague on 8 May 1945. Only then, could the Communist party take advantage of the situation, and Prague had its ad hoc city council and a Communist mayor.

It became clear that the transition from wartime fascism to democracy in Czechoslovakia would be complicated, if not impossible.

1

DEMOCRACY RE-STRUCTURED, 1945–46

As President Beneš finally arrived at the Hradčany castle in Prague to rule Czechoslovakia, he was heading a state whose power basis he did not know, and whose structures were established often against his wishes and intentions. He was back in power, thanks to the victory of the Red and American armies, but his power seems to have rested on the control of the 'unknown national committees' and Czech army units, which had returned to the country almost entirely from the USSR. However precarious his power might have seemed, the President retained immense international and domestic prestige to enable him to influence decisively subsequent development in Czechoslovakia. Above all else, he had international recognition as President by the Western Allies and Stalin himself; this made him acceptable to the Czech and Slovak Communists. Next, he had held great legislative and executive powers, and did not hesitate to use them. His international presitage permitted him to solve the age-long German problem; at Potsdam the victorious powers recognised the justice of the Czechoslovak claim aginst the Sudeten Germans, and agreed to their transfer to Germany. This particular success, soon to prove a grave political error, made the President acceptable to every Czech, except a handful of collaborators with the Germans.

As with the national committees, the President attempted to transform a spontaneous movement to punish collaborators and Germans on the spot, which invariably led to lynching or abuses, into something resembling justice. His retribution decree defined the crime of collaboration and set up tribunals to deal with the accused. This did check the most flagrant abuses, and in time eliminated summary justice. At the same time, it made the President strong enough to enable him to intervene in the administration of justice, if he thought that the spontaneous element was getting the upper hand. Thus, on the President's intervention, a former Minister of Justice, Dr. Kalkus, who had served in the Czech government during the war, was freed.

Under pressure from the left and due to chaotic conditions, President Beneš also had to make far-reaching decisions in the economy of Czechoslovakia. A series of presidential decrees nationalised all the mines, many industrial enterprises, most of the food industry, all the banks and insurance companies. On 19 May 1945, all German-owned and 'collaborationist' industrial enterprises were confiscated by another presidential decree; they were put under 'national management'. By August 1945, some 9,045 factories were administered under this arrangement, which meant roughly that they were nationalised. On 21 June 1945, President Beneš issued a decree, by which confiscated land was given to Czech and Slovak smallholders; this decree released some 3 million hectares for chiefly landless agricultural labourers. All these measures indicated that Beneš's presidential rule was vigorous, without any challenge, and as long as he remained in charge, Czechoslovakia would be a democratic state engaged in social experiments comparable to that of President Masaryk before the war.

In autumn 1945, Beneš was unanimously re-elected President by the unrepresentative Provisional National Assembly. But in June 1946, the freely elected parliament (Constituent National Assembly) also renewed his mandate unanimously. Unfortunately almost immediately after his re-election the President's health broke down.

The government, which shared executive power with the President, was appointed by Dr Beneš at Košice in April 1945 and was a coalition. Four Czech and two Slovak political parties were represented in it by their political leaders, who had managed to survive the war abroad, or who had risen into prominence in the Slovak revolt. It was a curious government, politically very finely balanced, but totally dependent on the President's wishes and whims, corresponding to no political reality on the ground. Recognising the liberation of Czechoslovakia by the Soviet armies, Beneš magnanimously granted the Czechoslovak Communist party a greater share of power than its pre-war strength would warrant. Its leader, K. Gottwald, was Deputy Prime Minister and the Communists also controlled the important ministries of the Interior, Education, Information and Agriculture. In addition the Slovak Communist leader, V. Široký, was also a Deputy Prime Minister and V. Clementis State Secretary in the Ministry of Foreign Affairs. Since the Prime Minister, Z. Fierlinger, was a left Social Democrat, who would never hesitate to join the Communists, the government seemed heavily tilted to the left. However, on closer examination it became obvious that in the case of a conflict the

Communists could paralyse the government, but could not defeat their coalition partners against the wishes of Beneš. Two key ministries (Defence and Foreign Affairs) were controlled by two prestigious non-party men, General L. Svoboda and Jan Masaryk, son of the first President of Czechoslovakia. In addition, several important ministries were under non-Communist control: Finance was controlled by a Slovak Democrat (I. Pictor), Justice and Foreign Trade by National Socialists (J. Stránský and H. Rypka). It was clear that if the non-Communists maintained unity, they could easily outvote the Communists and left Social Democrats, for important policy decisions were made by the government collectively in a majority vote. However, even if the non-Communists split, there existed another constitutional safeguard to prevent the Communists and their allies from seizing power.

The political government in Czechoslovakia has always left the administration of its policies to professional civil servants. These were traditionally politically neutral, and on the whole above party politics. Else they were members of non-Communists parties. The Communist party made little headway in the civil service: thus, for example, in the Ministry of Foreign Affairs only 6 out of 68 top officials were Communist party members; in the Ministry of Education only 19 out of 105; in the Ministry of Justice 3 out of 10 and in the Ministry of Foreign Trade 1 out of 82. While the Minister of the Interior, V. Nosek, was a Communist, General Bartík, who was in charge of the state security section, was replaced by Captain Pokorný, a Communist, only in 1946. The Communist minister, to make any headway, had to form new branches and invent new task forces (his Special Battalion was, however, disbanded in 1946) to put his political friends in charge of them (Border Guard Battalion), thus increasing only slowly communist influence in his ministry. Still, even then he could not really rely on these untried forces, in case he wanted to use them as his party's 'troops'. Furthermore, many security officers on the staff of the Ministry of the Interior were either non-Communists or openly anti-Communists and would not go away; they were unsackable civil servants. Judging from this uneasy balance of power in a key ministry, it could be said that the coalition partners were condemned to govern together.

The Communist party of Czechoslovakia, the principal partner of the ruling coalition, before it would even contemplate seizing power, had to be well organised and well led; boost its membership depleted by the war and win decidedly all the political battles lying ahead, such as parliamentary election in 1946 and 1948. Since his return

Gottwald, full of Soviet experience, devoted much care to securing his position as leader and paid much attention to building up party structure, the apparat. The leaders, who were notoriously divided in pre-war days, sorted out this problem as early as 8 April 1945 at Košice. At this early conference K. Gottwald was confirmed as leader-chairman, the Slovak leader, K. Šmidke, became vice chairman and R. Slánský remained Secretary General in charge of the party apparat. In reality this clearcut division of power within the party, made effective leadership as uncertain as before. On the Czech side, Gottwald had his own men elected to the central committee (Harus, Kopecký, Krosnář, Lastovička, Nosek, J. Procházka, M. Švermová). But the Slovaks remained unpredictable, with G. Husák and L. Novomeský openly separatist. To be really in charge in Prague, Gottwald had to 'exile' Šmidke, Husák and Novomeský to Slovakia: Šmidke became Speaker of the Slovenská národná rada (Provincial Parliament) and Husák Prime Minister (Predseda Sboru poverenníkóv). Slovaks transferred to Prague were V. Široký, who became the Slovak Communist party's chairman and J. Ďuriš, who became member of the Slovak praesidium. They were both Gottwald's men; they moved to Prague to represent Slovakia in the centre, but really to be Gottwald's pawns, who often encouraged the alcoholic leader in his radicalism. With the leadership uncertainties ostensibly solved, the party launched a massive membership drive, in view of winning the scheduled election.

The Communist party took full advantage of the liberation by the Red Army to organise itself on the spot. In June 1945, when the war was over and there was time for counting up, the party could claim some 597,500 members in the Czech and Slovak provinces; in Slovakia, the party said it had 197,277 members. No other party could come up with comparable figures. In any case the non-Communist parties never organised their supporters in the same manner as the communist party. They rather mobilised their followers for elections, than for membership. However, citizens' enthusiasm for joining the communist party began to wane soon after the launching of the drive, particularly in Slovakia. On the other hand, party membership continued to grow steadily in the Czech provinces. In August 1945 the Czech party had some 712,000 members; early in 1946, an additional 292,000 members were recruited and in March 1946, at the party congress in Prague, some 1,039 delegates represented 1,081,544 members. Of these, 58 per cent were workers, 13 per cent farmers and curiously some 50,000 artisans and tradesmen had joined the party as well. The party published six daily newspapers, with an estimated circulation of 700,000 and nineteen weeklies (circulation 150,000). During the congress, Gottwald proclaimed his satisfaction with the political performance of the party; it had over a million members, well organised in territorial units and would undoubtedly 'succeed' in the coming election.

Of the other parties, the best organised was the Slovak Democratic Party. It took part in the Slovak uprising, acting throughout as senior partner to Slovak Communists. The Democratic party held its congress even before the Communists, in April 1945, and at Košice its leaders obtained important ministries in the central government, as well as in the Slovak autonomous parliament and government. Although the Democratic party was in a minority in local and district committees (národní výbory), it, nevertheless, succeeded in gaining the confidence of the non-party majorities in these bodies. Thus it was quietly certain that it would do well in the coming election.

The three non-Communist Czech parties were all in bad shape. The war had dispersed their leaderships and completely destroyed their organisations. In 1945 they all had to start from scratch. The largest of them, the National Socialists, was by then a most peculiar amalgam of parties and social groups, if compared to its compact shape before the war. Historically, in the late 19th century, it was originally the nationalist splinter group of the Social Democratic party. However, during the years of the first Republic (1918–1939), the party's membership changed. The majority were no longer workers, but small businessmen, shopkeepers and professional people (civil servants, doctors, lawyers). Even before the war the party was disunited, had two wings, was badly led; but the factional friction within redoubled after the war, when the party attempted to absorb the outlawed parties, especially the National Democrats and Agrarians. P. Zenkl, leader of the right wing, had only just returned from the Buchenwald concentration camp, and was endorsed as party leader in February 1947. He had previously joined the government (1946) displacing the leader of the left wing elements, J. David. Fortunately for the party, David became Speaker of the newly elected Constitutional Assembly; even the Communist party voted for him. The Secretary General of the party became V. Krajina, formerly a National Democrat, who distinguished himself during the war fighting the Germans in the underground movement. Krajina concentrated on the administration and running of the party machine, which needless to say, was different from that of the Communist party and geared to pursue democratic aims.

Krajina's aim was a well-organized party, with a massive representation in the Assembly and top ministries in the government.

However, he never conceived the party as an instrument to the seizure of power, though his own left wingers often uttered such suspicions. In any case the left wing was able to put an effective brake on Krajina's fictitious aims. They argued that, in a democratic system, the party should have only loose structures and should concentrate on propagation of its policies and mobilisation of its followers (rather than members) for elections. Their arguments were endorsed by the party congress held in Prague on 28 February 1947. Some 3,000 delegates gathered at Prague-Vinohrady, a suburban stronghold of the party, and in the euphoria generated by this first postwar congress, seem to have achieved unity: the leaders of the right and left, Zenkl and David, kissed symbolically. However, the reality was different; the left wing retained control of all the important party committees and increased its representation by having Dr Šlechta, who led the party after the Communist coup, elected to the praesidium. The right wing failed to make their presence and influence felt, although Zenkl became leader and Krajina remained as Secretary General. As it was, the National Socialist Party could compete for power alongside the other parties, but could not hope to become a counterpart of the Communist Party in a power struggle.

The other Czech party, the People's Party, was in a similar position to that of the national socialists. It had never been an organised body but rather an association of voters with ideological (religious) links. Its leaders, Msgr Šrámek and Rev. Hála, were aging prewar personalities, and one could hardly speak of their leadership. The party was also split into factions. Though it attracted a lot of support from dissolved conservative parties, its rising young leaders were often radical mavericks, prepared for political compromises even with their ideological opponents, the Communists. Its strength lay in its appeal to cogent social groups (farmers, conservative professions and the middle class in general), who would always vote for it, thus making it a relatively strong party, but never the strongest nor capable of challenging the Communist party. It was a perfect coalition partner, which in prewar days had always been able to compromise with a coalition partner, be it communist or not.

The last of the Czech parties, the Social Democratic Party, like the Communist Party, had a compact following among workers, and historically was the senior Socialist Party. It emerged from the war rather battered, both in leadership and organisation. The provisional leader, Z. Fierlinger, held such far left views that many of the right wing comrades suspected him of being a Communist. The right wing itself was virulent but undistinguished, and only balanced out the left wing; the party did not disintegrate only thanks to its centrist group, which took over the leadership after the congress at Brno in the autumn of 1947. A. Laušman routed Fierlinger in the struggle for chairmanship of the party, but only in words and votes. Laušman's job as minister went to a left winger, while, within the party machine, the right wing Secretary General, B. Vilím, kept the centrists out of it. Thus, while the party was split at the top, it was depleted at its base; the post-war wave of revolutionary enthusiasm caused many Social Democrats to join the Communist Party. Still, in the post-war Czechoslovak system it was a decisive element; whomsoever it supported, would be the majority.

2

DEMOCRATIC ELECTIONS

With all the political parties fully aware of their strength, but not of their weakness, the coalition arrangement (and the National Front agreement) seems to have suited everyone. The non-Communist parties could only seriously rival the Communist Party if they united themselves internally and externally, which was well nye impossible. Otherwise they had to acquiesce to the increase in Communist influence, which they did. In August 1945, President Beneš appointed a Provisional National Assembly (a kind of parliament) in which every registered party obtained forty seats. This meant that the Communist Party of Czechoslovakia controlled a majority in this assembly, for it obtained forty seats for both Czech and Slovak branches as well as the majority of the forty seats reserved for social organizations (trade unions, veterans, youth league, etc.) This parliamentary strength was quite out of proportion to its pre-war electoral performance, but no one dared to raise their voice against it. It was thought that the imbalance would be put right after the parliamentary election, scheduled for May 1946.

The election, to be absolutely free, had to take place after the withdrawal of the occupation armies, the Red and American ones. Curiously, not these external factors, but the domestic ones, made the election less free than was customary in Czechoslovakia. While the armies withdrew peacefully, without interfering in the election campaign, the Czech and Slovak concensus on the banning of many pre-war political parties, particularly the strongest one, the Agrarian party, constituted the gravest interference in the freedom of vote. Only four Czech and four Slovak parties, all approved by the new National Front, were allowed to put forward candidates to the electorate, which then could choose to vote for them in a direct and secret ballot. It was expected that the voters of the prohibited parties would swell the non-Communist vote, and these parties would win a resounding victory. In a short but crisp campaign, the National Socialists and the People's Party made use of former Agrarian politicians to sway the electors their way, and convince them that they would represent their interests, but this blandishment worked in Slovakia only. The Communist Party appealed to the electors in a direct and most effective way: it declared itself responsible for the confiscation of German industrial and land property which was distributed among Czechs and Slovaks; thus it was in their interest to vote communist. It proposed further social reforms and experiments and, to everyone's surprise, emerged from the election as the largest political party of Czechoslovakia.

On 26 May 1946, the combined Czech and Slovak Communist Parties polled 2,695,293 votes, giving it 114 seats out of the 300. This was undoubtedly a victory, but not a decisive one. The other parties did badly: the National Socialist Party polled only 1,298,980 (18.3 per cent) votes; the People's Party 1,111,009 (15.6 per cent); the Slovak Democratic Party 999,980 (14.1 per cent) and the Social Democrats 955,539 (12.1 per cent). Although, in Slovakia, the Communist Party polled only some 30.3 per cent, and therefore became a minority party in that province. In the two Czech provinces, Bohemia and Moravia, the Communist Party had a small majority. On the whole, the communists, despite brave words, were disappointed; the Constituent Assembly, which was to draft a new constitution was as deadlocked as the Provisional one. Thus, in spite of best hopes, this election settled nothing and the uneasy coalition had to go on.

Nonetheless, the election results had an important effect on provincial and district councils (národní výbory) which they, in a sense, legitimised. In these councils (local government) the majority Communist Party consolidated 'democratically' its position, gained in the chaotic revolutionary post-war days. In the Czech provinces, the Communist Party had an absolute majority in 37.5 per cent of local councils (místní národní výbory); it had overall control in 55.1 per cent local councils and in 78 per cent district councils (okresní národní výbory). This advance was only partially offset at the provincial level: though the Communist Party retained control of the Bohemian provincial council, (zemský národní výbor) it lost control in Moravia and Slovakia. Of the 163 district councils, the Communist Party controlled 128, which seemed a fair recompense for the loss of the two provinces, since the provinces were under the direct jurisdiction of central government anyway. There, through the Interior Ministry they controlled them administratively.

ROAD TO A COMMUNIST COUP

Though clearly disappointed, as soon as the election was over, coalition partners got back to the day to day running of the country. Nonetheless, all attention was now centered on the next election, scheduled for May 1948. Provided that the same rules were in force then, one or the other party would gain a more decisive victory. For, up to then, the communist leaders never tired of repeating that there was a 'Czechoslovak way to communism', which undoubtedly meant that they would respect the democratic rules on their way to power.

However, soon it became obvious that the Communist Party was much more encouraged by the relative good electoral score than the other parties. It was made public during a central committee meeting on 22–23 January 1947: Gottwald said that his party's new objective was to win the scheduled election in 1948 decisively (51 per cent) and govern the country alone. The other parties refused to pay attention to such pronouncements, though retrospectively historians claim that as early a January 1947 the Communist Party decided to stage a coup d'Etat to obtain absolute power in Czechoslovakia. It seems more probable that this was a tactical move to test the nerve and determination of the non-Communists. At this time, the congress of the National Socialist Party confirmed its anti-Communist line. Shortly afterwards, at the Social Democratic Party congress, the left wing was decisively beaten, the party set out to divest itself of Communist influence and began to co-operate openly with non-Communist parties. If this type of regroupement of the democratic forces continued, the Communists could not hope to win the coming election.

Anti-Communist mood began to manifest itself in other spheres of life. Thus, for example, various courts began to annul confiscation decrees of industrial enterprises issued by Communist-dominated local or district authorities. The courts ordered these enterprises to be denationalised and handed over to their rightful owners. While the Communists successfully resisted the actual hand over by means of strikes and demonstrations, they could not prevent legal proceedings from continuing and ultimately the Czech and Slovak owners reclaiming their confiscated property. Communist influence in agriculture was also skillfully thwarted. In its election manifesto the Communist party wanted to confiscate and distribute all the land of estates over fifty hectares. On 1 July 1947 the Constituent Assembly passed a bill (Land Reform Act) which did not contain Communist proposals.

However, the Communist Party scored its own victories as a kind of encouragement on its way to the election of 1948. Thus, the struggle for the so-called millionaires' tax to finance subsidies for farmer' crops damaged by the drought in the summer of 1947 was won by thumbs up. When the party proposed that all citizens with property in excess of one million crowns should pay a special tax levy, as their contribution to the agricultural relief fund, the non-Communist majority in the government blocked the proposal (9 September 1947). The Communist Party then launched a propaganda campaign and proceeded to split the rank and file opinion of the other parties on this issue. On 10 September 1947, under pressure from its own camp, the government reversed its decision, the tax was enacted and some 4,000 million crowns in compensation were paid out to the farmers

What was more ominous than these domestic skirmishes, was the outbreak of the cold war in the international sphere. In June 1947, the Czechoslovak government was invited to participate at the European conference to decide on the allocation of American economic aid to Europe, the Marshall Plan. The government at first accepted the invitation, but after a visit to Moscow, Premier Gottwald declined to attend. Gottwald explained to his government colleagues that the USSR-Stalin promised to furnish Czechoslovakia with all the aid it needed. As a consequence of the drought, Czechoslovakia asked immediately for grain and fodder, and the USSR promptly agreed to send relief.

Another external political event helped to harden the political situation in Czechoslovakia. After a series of violent strikes, the Communist Party of France was excluded from a government coalition against which the strikes were directed. Czechoslovak Communists took the French events as a recipe for other European countries to follow. Their suspicions deepened, especially after the National Socialist leader, P. Zenkl, visited France and had talks with French socialist leaders. The visit was purely coincidental and similar tactics could simply not be employed in Czechoslovakia. On the other hand, in September 1947, Czechoslovak Communists attended a Cominform consultative meeting in Poland and it is equally unlikely that the future coup d'Etat in Czechoslovakia was discussed there. However, all these international events began to complicate internal politics. By then it became increasingly obvious that the intensified struggle for supremacy would be resolved even before the 1948 election.

In September 1947, the Communist Party staged a successful coup de force in Slovakia to tilt the balance of power its own way, in spite of the lost election. On 14 September 1947, the Slovak Ministry of the Interior, controlled by the provincial premier, G. Husák, announced that it had discovered a plot against Czechoslovakia, in which Slovak Democratic leaders were implicated. Two secretaries of the Slovak Democratic Party, Kempný and Bugár, were arrested and other leaders implicated in the affair were forced to resign (Deputy Premier in the central government, J. Ursíny). On 11 October 1947, the praesidium of the Slovak Communist Party met and decided to exploit the 'plot' politically and force the Slovak Democratic provincial ministers, who had nothing to do with the affair, to resign as well. On 30 October 1947, they swiftly convened a congress of factory councils which called for Democratic Party resignations. On the following day, the whole Slovak provincial government resigned and the National Front coalition asked the old Premier, G. Husák, to reconstruct the government. While Husak was supposed to consider a reshuffle, Slovak trade unions staged an hour strike to help him in his considerations. On 14 November, a peasant commission congress also urged Husák to purge the government of 'treacherous' elements. It is true that counter-demonstrations were organised by the Democratic Party at Bratislava, Košice and Zvolen, but they failed to impress public opinion, as they were not given publicity. On 18 November 1947, Husák announced the composition of the new provincial government which was most promptly approved by the central government: out of the fifteen ministers, members of the majority Democratic Party, Husák retained only five. The purge was constitutional, successful and the Communist Party had turned its 1946 electoral defeat into a great victory.

The smoothness of this coup de force must have influenced the Czechoslovak Communist leadership in Prague in its appreciation of the political situation. The Slovaks argued that, if a suitable pretext for similar purges could be found in Prague, their tactics could be followed nationwide: political opponents intimidated by strikes, demonstrations and public meetings could be removed from power and a political crisis could be resolved in a similar constitutional manner, without disturbing international public opinion. Though it still is not admitted, Communist decisions were probably made at this stage. On 28 November 1947, during another central committee meeting Premier Gottwald declared rather superfluously that the Communist Party 'would not be kicked out of power'. The declaration was not taken at all seriously, because every one in the country, even the bitterest opponents of Communism, knew full well that the Communist party could not be eliminated without a bloody civil war. However, by then it became evident to the Communist Party that it would not win 51 per cent of the votes in the coming election. Curiously an early opinion poll confirmed that the party would rather lose support than gain it. Gottwald issuing warnings to his opponents was in fact preparing the party for a crisis.

Since the other parties were increasingly confident that they would win the coming election they were unprepared, when the communist provoked crisis did come. If they had any tactics to resist the communist coup de force it was a constitutional one: after a Communist defeat in the cabinet or in the Assembly, where they had majorities, the deadlock would be resolved by the President in appointing a cabinet of experts and holding an earlier election. This tactic was never fully worked out and there was no consensus on it among the non-Communist parties. The communists moved first and forced the non-Communists to provoke the crisis themselves. On 10 February 1948, the Social Democratic minister, V. Majer, presented a proposal at the government meeting by which the higher grades of the civil service should get substantial salary increases. The Communist Minister of Finance, J. Dolanský, rejected this proposal, but the government, which always approved policies and financial measures collectively by a majority vote, over-ruled Dolanský. Constitutionally, the minister had to implement a measure which he and presumably the Communist Party did not approve. This important government meeting at which the Communist Party was defeated, was attended, for some reason, by A. Zápotocký, chairman of the Trade Union Council (Ústřední rada odborů) and member of the Communist Party praesidium. Most significantly, he also disagreed with the salary increases and there and then decided on extra-governmental and parliamentary means to block the proposal. He persuaded the TUC to convoke a congress of all the workers councils and trade unions, on 22 February 1948, to approve his decisions.

Zápotocký's protest gesture, although it came so shortly after the events in Slovakia, did not appear particularly ominous, since it seemed inconceivable that it could lead to a coup under such trivial pretext. It was rather considered as a move to divide the opponents: several non-Communist trade union leaders (National Socialist Krejčí and Social Democrat Cipro) as well as rank and file members opposed the governments decision. Subsequent events proved that it was part of a concerted communist attempt at a coup.

On the contrary, the non-Communists, encouraged by their 'show of unity' in outvoting the communists in the government, decided to press on their advantage and embarrass Communist ministers and Premier Gottwald even more. The National Socialist deputy, Hora, member of the security committee of the Constituent Assembly, learned about a transfer of eight police officers from the forces to administrative duties. It appeared to be a routine move, but Hora rightly decided otherwise. He informed his party ministers, Drtina and Ripka, about this ominous measure: all the officers were members of the National Socialist Party. The ministers decided to raise the matter at the next meeting of the government, scheduled for 13 February. This meeting was to discuss the social security bill, but on the insistence of the non-Communist ministers police matters were put on the agenda instead, although the Minister of the Interior, V. Nosek, was sick and could not attend. After prolonged and heated discussion, the non-Communist ministers scored another 'voting victory': Nosek was instructed to put the police matters right and cancel transfers. The Communist Party, however, took this as a declaration of war leading to a final showdown.

As the Zápotocký episode showed, the Communist Party had already mobilised their supporters in the trade unions for the congress. Now it decided to mobilise supporters among the farmers, and called for a congress to be held in Prague shortly after the trade unions. The party itself had been apparently in a state of readiness since November 1947, while the non-Communists had only just begun their preparations: consultations did take place, but no common action was agreed upon. On 16 February 1948, the National Socialist leaders gathered and seemingly took the decision to resign from the government, if Nosek refused to implement the government's decision on police transfers. The following day, the National Socialist leaders met the Peoples Party leadership as well as the right wing Social Democrats, and agreed to insist on the implementation of the police decision at whatever cost. What they had in mind were resignations of all non-communist ministers from Gottwald's government and a nice constitutional crisis to be resolved by the President. They failed to call on their supporters to organise counter-protests and counter-meetings. It was thought sufficient for the non-Communist ministers to obstruct the cabinet meeting, offer the President their resignations and force Gottwald himself to resign as Premier. On 19 February 1948, numerous communist meetings took place all over the country and telegrams of protest 'at the reactionary activity of government ministers' were sent to all political leaders, the President included.

Another government meeting was scheduled for 20 February 1948, which was to be attended by the Minister of the Interior. National Socialist, People's Party and the Slovak Democratic ministers met in the office of the Deputy Premier, P. Zenkl, who telephoned Gottwald enquiring about the police measures. On receiving a negative answer, they all decided to boycott the meeting. Later that day they submitted their resignations from the government to the President. This was the limit to their action; after that, it was the turn of the President and the Communists.

The following day, Premier Gottwald attended a huge meeting in the centre of Prague, at which he analysed the political crisis for the crowds and the country: "the counter-revolutionary reaction had tried to overthrow the people's democratic regime. They failed, but as a result they would be ejected not only from the government but from power altogether". Gottwald then asked his followers to form purge committees (akční výbory) all over the country and expel all the 'reactionaries' from whatever office they may hold. Husák, the Slovak Premier, immediately asked the five Democratic Party ministers to resign in Slovakia. With a nationwide purge set in motion and the consequent panic, only the President could solve the crisis constitutionally. However, the President was by now under sustained pressure to accept the resignations of the non-Communist ministers and allow Gottwald to reshuffle the government. On 22 February, the trade unions congress exerted its pressure on the ailing President: apart from passing resolutions calling for more nationalisation, land reform and modified civil service salary increases, it announced an hour token general strike in support of Premier Gottwald.

On 23 February, political chaos became evident although the President continued to hold out. In Slovakia, Husák's new purged government contained no official leaders of the Democratic Party and was dominated by the Communists. Purges at all levels were in full swing, although the central purge organisation (ústřední akční výbor národní fronty) had only just been created. Next day, the general strike was complete and, for an hour, the country came to a standstill. In Prague the Communist Party staged continuous meetings in the streets and in Wenceslas Square. This was obviously the climax of the crisis. If the non-Communists would not admit defeat, they had to reply with counter-demonstrations.

But they were all surprised by the turn of events. This was not the constitutional confrontation they had prepared for, and they were at a loss what to do next. The National Socialist leaders were not even in Prague; Zenkl and Ripka had left for the provinces to address party meetings. In these tense circumstances the People's party cracked up first; its ailing leader, Msgr. Šrámek, failed to control his left wing which agreed to join Gottwald's coalition government. After that the party leadership desintegrated, not waiting for the final solution of the crisis. Next Slovak Democrats panicked and their left wing took over the party: they renamed it the Slovak Renaissance Party. In this confusion, the Social Democrats were not told of the resignations, although its ministers strongly supported the non-Communists on the police matters. The party as a whole decided not to resign from the government, thus making Gottwald's survival quite constitutional.

Only on 25 February 1948, did a flicker of hope rise and fade away: non-Communist students in Prague marched to the Hradčany palace in support of the President. This was the only demonstration in support of the non-Communists; it was relatively small, came too late and was easily dispersed by the police, without much bloodshed. With the mass meeting continuing in Wenceslas Square, Gottwald, Nosek and A. Zápoctocký arrived at the Hradčany castle to see the President and present him with a list of ministers for the reconstructed government. After an hour's negotiation, with the roar of the Communist demonstration in Wenceslas Square clearly audible, the President yielded, accepted the resignations and appointed the new government in due constitutional form. Although the new government had to be approved by the Constituent Assembly as well, the President's decision really ended the crisis and put a constitutional seal on the communist coup. In the great panic which struck Czechs and Slovaks during the crisis, the Communists were able to take over the state administration, local government, universities, social organisations and the non-Communist parties themselves. The army remained neutral, the police was hardly used, the takeover being political. Czechoslovak democracy was destroyed solely by organised street demonstrations and panic that followed; nationwide purges accomplished its destruction. This process demonstrated its vital flaw: political parties could only make use of the democratic system, but the entire people had to defend it. Since the non-communists could not mobilise people in its defence, the system failed. Paradoxically, in 1989, the Communists would be victims to the same process.

The newly-confirmed Prime Minister, K. Gottwald, went directly from the royal castle, the President's seat, to Wenceslas Square, and announced his final victory to the crowd which went hysterical with joy. On that very day, non-Communist leaders rapidly dispersed, escaping abroad into exile, leaving the Communists and their allies to complete the power takeover peacefully, The Constituent Assembly, thoroughly intimidated, approved the new government overwhelmingly (230 votes out of 300). A deadly calm returned to Czechoslovakia after the excitement of the crisis. Public order was never disturbed.

Even the United Nations could not demonstrate that a violent revolution with Soviet help had taken place in Czechoslovakia. Gottwald acted on his own and the coup d'Etat became a model for other communist parties. Without even Gottwald suspecting it, the real revolutionary upheaval came about a year later.

3

THE DISSOLUTION OF DEMOCRATIC CZECHOSLOVAKIA

Premier Gottwald set into motion a nation-wide purge, even before he had obtained the constitutional sanction from President Beneš to re-constitute his government. The twelve ministers, 'who had revolted against him', were finally sacked. However, his general call on 21 February, for the formation of 'action committees' to purge the country of 'reactionaries and traitors', had to be made more concrete. On 23 February, the Central Action Committee met to interpret Gottwald's call and give it substance. It turned itself into a central purge 'tribunal', presided over by the trade union leader, A. Zápotocký; its executive secretary was Gottwald's son-in-law, A. Čepička. It consisted of ninety-three members who were overwhelmingly Communist; non-Communist parties were also represented on it, though only by individual members. On 5 March, fifteen representatives of the Slovak Action Committee of the National Front were added to this central organisation to establish its jurisdiction in that province. This central tribunal set about its work immediately: it purged the Constitutent Assembly, central administration, including ministries, and the leaderships of political parties. As 'action committees' were formed at all levels, in the provinces and districts as well as locally in factories, industrial enterprises, universities and schools, newspaper offices and printing works, theatres and social organisations, they also began to purge 'reactionaries' on their levels.

Gottwald's vagueness about 'reactionaries and traitors' caused some difficulties. It was not difficult to purge 'reactionaries' in factories and industrial enterprises, where local communists argued there were few of them. Since they were mainly workers, how could you purge them? In such places, therefore, the Communist Party turned the purge into a membership drive; it dissolved the branches of the other parties and invited members to join the party. At Zlín (subsequently Gottwaldov and after 1989 again Zlín) in the Baťa shoe enterprise, the party's membership jumped overnight from 9,658 to 11,407; at Pilsen, the Škoda works branch increased its membership from 9,771 to 11,220; at Jinonice, the Walter Works branch from 1,070 to 1,334.

Curiously, the central administration did not present many problems either, though it contained most of the 'reactionaries' Gottwald must have referred to. The government itself was purged with utmost ease. The ministers, who had resigned, left their departments peacefully, before the final resolution of the crisis, usually under pressure from the purge committees which were formed in each ministry, mostly from ancillary personnel (porters, cleaning staff, etc.). One minister (V. Majer) refused to leave his office and was physically ejected from it, presumably by the purge committee. With the ministers went also 28,000 civil servants, who were magnanimously allowed to join the industrial labour force. State administration never recovered from this loss of expertise and proved inefficient throughout the communist period in power.

The extent of the purge in public administration can best be gauged from the figures of Communist Party membership in the various ministries. Thus, in the Ministry of Agriculture, which throughout 1945–49 had a Communist minister, J. Ďuriš, only some 11 per cent of civil servants were members of the party. By 1948, after the shock of the coup, 29 per cent were Communist Party members. However, in 1949, 79 per cent of civil servants in this ministry were party members. This meant that some 50 per cent of the civil servants were dismissed in 1948; the rest in the 1950s. The Ministry of Industry lost 352 of its civil servants between February and March 1948, while the Ministry of Post only 219, possibly because it remained under the control of a non-communist minister. By September 1948 central ministries dismissed some 1,525 civil servants and pensioned off 1,014 others. In Slovakia the purge on this level was less violent and only some 159 civil servants were dismissed, 47 pensioned off and 301 suspended. However, from the scale of dismissals it is clear that central administration was thoroughly disrupted. This must have been the Communist objective, for the party was determined to re-organise public administration and staff it with its own personnel.

Although the army played no active role in the coup d'Etat, the purge hit it in a devastating way. Immediately after the coup, 2,965 higher ranks (27.5 per cent) were dismissed from service. There the purge continued until 1950, by which time 60 per cent of the officer corps was replaced by handpicked communists. The party established nine special officers schools for factory workers and during 1948–49 these schools turned out 1,800 new officers. When in 1950 the army was re-organised and re-equipped, even its post-war leader, the self-proclaimed secret communist, General L. Svoboda, was dismissed and replaced by Gottwald's son-in-law, A. Čepička, a lawyer by profession. In the tiny security service, the purge went on smoothly; the few non-Communist officers either escaped abroad or were discreetly liquidated à la soviétique. Only in 1968 did these murders come to light, the victims rehabilitated and their executioners brought to justice. However, the Communist replacements did not survive in their posts either, since most of them were purged in 1950 and killed subsequently. On Soviet advice, a Ministry of Security was established and the services entirely restructured.

The purge affected equally severely local government, although most of it was under Communist control already. On 25 February 1948, the Minister of the Interior, V. Nosek, issued an instruction by which dismissals were sanctioned in the local government bodies. In the first month of the purge, some 25,000 local government personnel were dismissed. In July 1948, when appeals were allowed, of 15,000 who did appeal, ony 500 were upheld. The full extent of this purge is not known even today, but it is evident that all the local government councils (40,000) came under Communist control. In many cases entire councils had to be dissolved and replaced by lonely Communist individuals living in the locality. But on the whole, Communist councillors contented themselves with assuming the chairmanships of the councils; public order departments were invariably purged and taken over. Those local government officials, who after the war administered the councils, appointed as secretaries or as elected members, were also purged. Their jobs were taken over by local communist politicians in triumphant mood. But it is only a slight exaggeration to say that effective local administration ceased, and has never recovered since. On 1 January 1949, this heavily damaged administrative machine was 'completely reorganised': the administrative 'land' system (Bohemia, Moravia and Slovakia) was replaced by the regional system which divided Czechoslovakia into twenty regions, 160 districts and some 40,000 communes.

The destruction of the parliamentary system was also relatively easy. The Constituent Assembly was so intimidated by the coup d'Etat, that it voted overwhelmingly confidence to the new government. Only seventy deputies, out of three hundred, failed to take part in the proceedings: among the 230 confidence votes, the non-Communists were still in majority. They voted for Gottwald's government, knowing well that their vote meant the dissolution of the democratic system. In May 1948, the general election, conducted under a different electoral law, sealed its fate. It was no longer a parliament (in Czechoslovakia called the National Assembly), elected in a free election, in which political parties competed with each other for votes. It was now a parliament, but only in name, to which single candidates were nominated by the National Front, a communist dominated body. Thus, in May 1948, voters could only vote for such candidates; they could not even spoil their ballot papers, for they were 'encouraged' to vote in public: screens were missing in some election rooms. The National Front, which had existed before the coup, became the key body of the new system.

In this sort of election, it was natural that the National Front gave the Communist Party an overwhelming majority: 215 seats out of 300. The three Czech parties were assigned an arbitrary representation of twenty-three seats each, while the two Slovak parties obtained twelve and four seats respectively.

Thus, the supreme legislative body, the National Assembly, was dominated by the Communist Party, by means of a rigged election. The new power situation was legitimised by the new Constitution, which was promulgated at the same time. It was defined as a purely legislative body, many of its former powers transferred to its presidium. In fact, its powers now resembled strikingly those of the Supreme Soviet, although in name and shape it was the traditional Assembly. However, in 1949, a new procedural law further limited the powers of the individual members, and committees; plenary sessions took place twice a year approving unanimously and retrospectively all the legislation and decrees promulgated without debate by its presidium. In this way, this unique Assembly became a copy of its Soviet counterpart.

Elsewhere, the purge dealt a terrible blow to the judiciary. The Communists considered it, rather naively, the most 'reactionary profession of the defeated bourgeoisie'. The Ministry of Justice was under non-Communist control since 1945, and the Communists had hardly any members among the civil servants and judges. The minister, P. Drtina, purged himself, attempting to commit suicide. An action committee then purged the ministry. The administration of justice was immediately simplified. The constitutional court, together with the supreme administrative court, were abolished. The former verified the validity of elections and became superfluous; the latter judged cases arising from conflicts between citizens and administration. It was argued that, since the working class was in power, it could not be in conflict with itself. A great majority of professional judges were dismissed and replaced by handpicked workers. The Communist dean of the Law faculty at Prague University, J. Bartuška, admitted some 1,200 workers to special courses which after eighteen months of intensive training turned them into judges with academic diplomas. However, they had to practise their profession even before taking their degrees, as they were in great demand. Many of the purged were now accused of 'treason' and had to be dealt with. Subsequently, the sentences resulting in judicial murders were described as 'excesses of the cult of personality'.

The great panic, which seized the population at large consequent on the coup, is historically inexplicable. It enabled the Communist Party to take over even those institutions where it was hardly represented. Thus, at Brno University, Professor F. Trávníček, a philologist and the only prominent Communist on the staff, responded to the Central Action Committee's appeal on 25 February 1948 by declaring himself chairman of the University Purge Committee. On his initiative, the few party members in the four faculties formed their own purge committees, but in the law faculty he had to appoint one consisting of porters and students only. The committees purged the four elected leaders of the Students Unions, and expelled eighty-eight other students from the University; only eighteen members of staff were dismissed. But this mild shock tactics was sufficient to achieve communist objectives: the university's work went on without interruption and the Communist Party membership jumped up sixfold. In the autumn of 1948, when its power was stabilised, the party was able to really purge this 'reactionary institution': the law faculty expelled 45.5 per cent of its undergraduates, arts faculty 28.5 per cent, natural sciences 27.4 per cent, medical faculty 20.9 per cent and the Institute of Education 5 per cent. In 1950, the recalcitrant law faculty was dissolved, its students dispersed and the staff joined the Slavonic Institute. In exactly the same mild and almost casual way were purged the trade unions, Veteran Association (membership 153,506), Peasant Commissions, Women's Councils, Youth organisations and the Sokol Gymnast Association (membership 569,213) which despite 11,446 expulsions continued its defiance; it was simply absorbed by the Workers Gymnastic Association.

Necessarily special attention had to be paid to the purge of the non-Communist leadership and their parties. At the top purges were conducted by the new leaders, ministers, whom Gottwald selected for his reconstituted government. The Social Democratic Party seemed to have escaped the purges at first altogether. The chairman, E. Laušman, remained in office; only four members of the presidium were expelled, and the Secretary General suspended, because of ill health. However, at regional and district levels, Social Democrats were purged more severely. Then suddenly, on 11 March 1948, Laušman was dismissed and replaced by Z. Fierlinger. In May 1948, regional and district committees 'decided' to join their communist equivalents. Finally, on 27 June 1948, the Social Democratic Party fused with the Communist Party: four Social Democrats (Fierlinger, Jankovcová, John, Erban E.) were added to the Communist Party presidium and eleven others were co-opted in the central committee.

All the other non-Communist parties suffered complete destruction. The National Socialist Party's presidium contained only one dissident, A. Šlechta. Nonetheless, he was able to take over the party as a whole after the other leaders had fled abroad. Regional and district leaders also abandoned party offices (and possibly also the country whenever they were able to); thus, in fact the party dissolved itself. The new leaders also changed its name to the Czech Socialist Party; some members joined the Communist Party, others simply left politics altogether. Its membership slumped from 593,982 to some 20,000. In 1950, there were only 0.3 per cent of Czech Socialists active in public life.

In the People's Party, the destruction was more gradual, although its presidium disintegrated even before the purge. Its majority dispersed to avoid arrest. The party chairman, Msgr. Šrámek, was caught by the security police trying to escape from the country together with the Secretary General, Fr. Hála. They were both arrested and kept interned in a monastery, where they both died later. The leaders of the left wing faction, A. Petr and Fr. Plojhar, took over joining Gottwald's new government. The new Secretary General (also named Hála) refused to purge the party, but was quickly replaced by a more willing A. Pospíšil. After the election in 1948, in which many People's Party members voted against National Front candidates, Pospíšil was ordered to dismantle the party altogether. The party blamed the Catholic Church for the 'disloyalty vote' of its members. The Communist Party took advantage of this pseudo-conflict and destroyed them both. In 1950, only 2.3 per cent of People's Party members were still in public life.

In Slovakia, where the non-Communists were in the majority, the purge had to be even more ruthless than in the Czech provinces. The Democratic Party disintegrated on its own. It changed its name and its top leaders either escaped abroad, or joined the Slovak Communist Party. The latter example was emulated particularly at the district level, where entire committees joined the Communist Party. Twenty-two members of the Slovak National Council were expelled, thus enabling the Communist Party to have a majority in that body. The other Party of Freedom tried for a time to exploit the upheaval in the ranks of the Democratic Party and recruit them. However, the Communist-dominated Action Committees of the Slovak National Front stopped this poaching. Subsequently, the Party of Freedom once again receded into political insignificance. By 1950, all the Slovak non-Communist parties ceased to exist as organised bodies, although their leaders continued a precarious existence at the top in order to uphold the constitutional pretence that communist Czechoslovakia was the same as the democratic one.

In the economic sphere, the effects of the coup d'Etat were incalculable. By 1948, Czechoslovakia had achieved a relatively high standard of living and was much ahead in its recovery from war damage of all the East European countries, including the USSR, particularly in industrial production. On the completion of the Two Year Plan (1946–48), despite difficulties, Czechoslovak industry produced slightly more than in 1937, the last normal year before World War II. Although in heavy industrial goods production exceeded by one quarter that of 1937, in consumer goods it still lagged behind (79.8 per cent). The weakness of the Czechoslovak economy lay in agriculture: because of the drought in 1947 agriculture failed to reach its pre-war level and foodstuffs had to be imported. On the whole, however, it seemed that the country was heading towards prosperity in the near future.

After the coup, all industry was nationalised, with the exception of small enterprises which accounted for 15.9 per cent of industrial production. A new Five Year Plan was prepared to increase industrial production to 157 per cent and agricultural production to 154 per cent of the 1937 level; a significant rise in the standard of living was forecast. Rapidly it became evident that the new Plan was unrealistic. Nonetheless, the Plan was thoroughly discussed in the Planning Commission, the Communist Party and the National Assembly made it a law in October 1948.

From the very beginning, Czechoslovak Communist leaders worried about the Five Year Plan and above all about the concrete forecast of rising living standards. In November 1948, the central committees, therefore, decided to substitute it with a less concrete objective: "establishing socialism" in Czechoslovakia. Soon their misgivings proved right. The Plan went wrong almost at the time of its launch, and with it the rising standards of living. J. Goldman, one of the prominent economists concerned with the preparation of the Plan, dared to state publicly several reasons for its failure: 'the Plan was an amateurish affair which had many weaknesses, and the most fundamental one was that it did not secure raw material supplies, because they were outside

Czechoslovakia'. In 1949, he was arrested, accused of economic sabotage and imprisoned. But his criticism showed the folly of central planning in Czechoslovakia, which could not control its raw material supplies. The failure of the USSR and the Communist East European states to help Czechoslovakia with raw materials showed that central planning would be impossible for this part of Europe. Simultaneously with the Plan failure, Czechoslovakia's economy was plunged into steep inflation; consumer goods disappeared from the market; industrial development took an erratic turn. The country simply could not cope with the ideological and power-political victory of Communism and ultimately had to pay for it with living standards.

In agriculture, the decline was similar. Although its performance was not outstanding even before the coup d'Etat, this was not the fault of the farmers, but was largely due to the drought in 1947. However, an additional political factor seemed responsible for this lack of performance: farmers feared wholesale collectivisation on the Soviet pattern and held back investments. The Communist Party was aware of these fears and, since it drew sizeable support from the farmers (mainly from those who had benefitted from the land confiscations in 1945–46), attempted to deny these rumours as 'malicious inventions of the reactionaries'. However, the situation changed after the coup. Everybody now expected the party to carry out its ideological objectives in agriculture and collectivise it. Still the party hesitated. Since agriculture in Czechoslovakia was run mainly by small and medium farmers, and these farmers worked in highly developed co-operatives, it seemed reasonable to keep the system as it was, and improve it rather than dismantle it. The state began to establish and finance huge state farms and encouraged the formation of collective farms to increase land holdings and production. The Plan was going to make available capital investments to mechanise farmers and their co-operatives. Gottwald intended to delay wholesale collectivisation by three or more years. Ďuriš, Minister of Agriculture, demanded increased investments in his sector in the FYP. Then, in the autumn of 1948, difficulties with the purchases of agricultural produce arose in the country. The party, there and then, decided to solve problems ideologically. In 1949, a vigorous campaign of collectivisation was launched, but was fiercely resisted. Faced with this resistance, collectivisation had to be temporarily suspended in some regions. The choice was between an uninterrupted production and wholesale collectivisation. Again, for ideological reasons, the party opted for the latter. This choice could not have come at a more inconvenient time; with the erratic performance of industry Czechoslovakia could not buy as much foodstuffs from abroad as it had need for. Henceforth the country suffered chronic food shortages and bread remained strictly rationed until 1953.

Thus between 1948 and 1953 Czechoslovakia underwent the most revolutionary transformation, which was not always for the good of the country. The new political system was really established towards the end of Gottwald's term in office in 1953. It was a carbon copy of the Stalinist model, in force in the USSR. The system, like that of Stalin, required a strong leader, which Gottwald was not. But he was the only Czechoslovak leader, who knew how to make it work. In a sense, Gottwald was fortunate that Czechoslovakia's constitution and tradition postulated a strong Presidency. Before him, the Presidents of Czechoslovakia, Professors Masaryk and Beneš, had great powers at their disposal, but used them sparingly, in emergencies only. In June 1948, after his 'election' as President, Gottwald made it clear that he would be a strong president. However, conditions in Czechoslovakia as well as in the other ideologically allied countries, above all the USSR, required tyrannical dictators, not strong democratic presidents. Thus, because of this historical quirk Gottwald became a Stalinist dictator organically: combined with the top party office the Presidency gave him constitutional powers to destroy the old system and create his own. He muzzled the National Assembly (already weakened by the new electoral law) and then transformed it into a ceremonial Supreme Soviet. He appointed a weak government, consisting mainly of his old political companions who, while politically skilful and experienced, could not administer the country; after the purge of the civil service and its virtual replacement by party picked amateurs, ministers were not only decision makers, as before, but also administrators–civil servants. This task was probably above any politician's capacity. Ostensibly Gottwald came to their rescue and took all decisions himself. He strengthened the presidential chancellory: presidential officials were appointed government ministers, trouble-shooters, political scientists, top civil servants and economic managers. Policy decisions were made in the party presidium, but that meant Gottwald again. In appearance Gottwald was as omnipotent as Stalin. But Stalin's system worked thanks to terror. Gottwald's system did not work, so he had to ask Stalin to send him advisor in terror to make it work. Paradoxically, terror, even with Soviet advisors, failed to work in Czechoslovakia as well. It disrupted still further the state, the economy and even the party. Nonetheless in 1953, when Stalin and Gottwald died, their successors instead of abolishing the Stalinist system and working out another one, abolished terror and hoped that the communist system would somehow work.

Given the presidential tradition, it was not surprising that Gottwald had much less trouble controlling the state than the party machine. It was easy to dominate the state as President and use it as his personal instrument of power. But the party secretariat, led by the capable Slánský, escaped his stranglehold, and if anything acquired more executive power than some of the ministries it tried to replace. Slánský himself concentrated his entire attention on national security. At the same time, he convinced his fellow leaders, Gottwald and Zápotocký, intellectual nonentities, that in Czechoslovakia it was necessary to plan everything centrally, to collectivise agriculture and re-organise the state and administration to resemble that of the USSR. As General Secretary, he was sure that his powers would increase and for a short time it seemed to be so. The party machine was solid and under Slánský's control, while, after the first stages of the radical reforms and reorganisations, the state and the economy, in fact lapsed into chaos and confusion. It appeared that Slánský and the party apparat would become more powerful than Gottwald and the presidium. Before this could become a reality, on Soviet advice, Gottwald eliminated Slánský: at first he appointed him Deputy Premier, then executed him as 'traitor'. Without Slánský the secretariat ceased to rival the presidency and became a purely administrative office.

The Communist Party's central committee also wanted greater powers in the changed circumstances. However, in the end Gottwald forced it to content itself with the trappings of power. It tried unsuccessfully to assume the role of the National Assembly: it wanted to formulate and vote party policies which now became state policies. But Gottwald, like Stalin, disliked it. Though the central committee held its meetings in the historical Vladislav Hall of the Prague royal castle, there its power writ stopped. In the end, it was allowed to meet and approve unanimously, without debate, the leader's decisions. In May 1949, Gottwald convoked the ninth congress of the Czechoslovak Communist Party, which most enthusiastically approved all the changes made in Czechoslovakia since the coup d'Etat. Gottwald's 'leading role' was also approved. The party machine was to be reorganised to be 'capable of governing': Soviet experience had to be utilised in this respect. As a result the Communist Party of Czechoslovakia became a copy of the Soviet party, whether the members wanted it or not. Gottwald also requested Stalin to send him experienced Soviet advisors to help with the reorganisation, especially in the field of security and the army. In turn, the central committee was transformed into a huge bureaucratic machine à la soviétique: departments were established to cover the whole gamut of national existence. They were responsible for everything on earth and reported directly to the leader, Gottwald. Even then to make quite sure that the central committee did not usurp too much power for itself, Gottwald convoked its sessions at irregular intervals: in 1948, after the coup, it met three times; in 1949 twice (to 'elect' the new leadership); in 1950 once; in 1951 three times and in 1952 once. Since Gottwald convoked the meeting of the presidium-politburo also only occasionally, the Czechoslovak Communist Party ceased to be a political body subject to its rules and statutes, and instead became the Stalinist bureaucratic machine retaining only the outer appearance of a political party. All power resided with President Gottwald—the party leader, who maintained himself in power by controlling the new security apparat and the army, managed for him by Soviet advisors. Practically nothing was left of the old Czechoslovakia and, to infuse some dynamism into this new Czechoslovakia, a vigorous application of Soviet type terror was necessary. As long as Stalin and Gottwald were alive, the 'machine' mysteriously kept on working. After their deaths, in 1953, Czechoslovakia was once again in flux.

The transformation of the Communist Party into a Party-State was a difficult task, even for Gottwald with his terror and deadly purges. It is probably true that Gottwald and the co-leaders did not particularly want to destroy a political system they knew so well, which worked well and which took them such great pains to make their own. It is now clear that Gottwald acted on Stalin's instructions, in deadly fear of the Soviet tyrant. In 1945, on his return from Moscow, Gottwald was quite sure that he wanted to return to the prewar, liberal democratic system, because Stalin told him so. There was a 'Czechoslovak way to socialism': he took that to mean that the party would come eventually to power democratically from within the Czechoslovak system. Only then, would it organically go on to 'the building of socialism', slightly altering the system, if at all.

Therefore, between 1945–48, the party's priority was mass membership and electoral victories. From the end of the war to the eighth congress in March 1946, the party succeeded in recruiting over one million members and emerged from the general election in June 1946 as the largest party in Czechoslovakia. After the election the recruitment went well, and by February 1948 there were some 1,400,000 registered members. The victorious coup opened the floodgates, and by May 1949 the party contained over two million members and candidates. Encouraged by the successful recruitment drive the party leadership launched a pre-election slogan in the autumn of 1947: it wanted to poll 51 per cent of the vote in the scheduled election. This was to be the first decisive electoral victory by any Communist party; the party would come to power through the ballot box; it would govern alone and implement its policies unhindered by any coalition partners. This seemed to be its tactics in 1947. Why by February 1948 the Communist Party carried out a 'constitutional' coup d'Etat is still a mystery, for this time Stalin had not ordered Gottwald anything. In fact, when Gottwald gained absolute power, albeit not through the ballot box, he tried to restrain him: constitutional appearances had to be kept for international reasons. However, the rapid growth in membership after the coup indicates that Gottwald himself was not sure of his position and still dreamt of a national majority to uphold his policy. The rigged election did not resolve his doubts. Only in September 1948 did the central committee get down to discussing the new members, and since it had no need for winning any more elections, it considered stopping it. It was argued that the social composition of the Communist Party had been so altered by the influx of new non-working class members that it would have to be purged as well.

However, something untoward must have happened during the summer 1948. After a holiday in the Crimea with Stalin, Gottwald came back to Czechoslovakia a changed man: he had been given precise instructions as to the future political system. Stalin ordered Gottwald bluntly to remodel the party and the state on the Soviet pattern. If he found the task too difficult, Stalin promised him 'fraternal help' in the form of Soviet advisors. After six months of trying on his own, Gottwald had to call for Soviet assistance. He thought that he kept the state under control, but could not cope with mounting economic problems, national security and the urgent party purge.

According to Gottwald the Communist Party had to be purged of 'undesirable' elements that infiltrated it after the coup. On the other hand the party and the state had to be fused to act as one. With the aid of Soviet advisors, Gottwald was so successful in achieving this aim that his successors were unable to disentangle the party from the state. Only in 1968 did the 'regeneration' movement, led by the new party leadership, announce its intentions to cut loose the party from the state. In August 1968 foreign intervention put a stop to the efforts.

4

COMMUNIST APPARAT

Before the coup d'Etat, the Communist Party's presidium was only a loose body: 11 ministers belonged to it *ex officio* and the secretary general, Slánský, prepared its agenda. It met irregularly and made decisions on immediate political problems facing the party. In April 1945, Gottwald's presidium consisted of six men only: Slánský, Gottwald's faithful companion and secretary; Kopecký, a demagogic orator who became Minister of Information in the first government of Czechoslovakia; V. Nosek, a trade unionist returning from Britain, who also became Minister of the Interior; and two Slovak Communists, Široký and Šmidke, both emerging from the Slovak uprising and therefore unknown quantities. Subsequently Gottwald added to the presidium J. Smrkovský, but quickly dropped him (May–June 1945); A. Zápotocký, his most assiduous companion; J. Dolanský, a university professor who became his economic and administrative brain; J. Ďuriš, Slovak who replaced Šmidke; J. Krosnář, another trade unionist; and M. Švermová, wife of Gottwald's companion killed in the war, who became secretary. However, when in March 1946 a large presidium was elected at the Eighth Congress, Gottwald got round its size by forming a narrow presidium: Kopecký, Dolanský, Zápotocký, Slánský and Široký, who was the only Slovak willing to listen to him. It was this narrow presidium which took the decision to carry out the coup d'Etat in 1948. The coup itself was carried out by Gottwald and certain ministers. Up to 1948 the inner circle was a co-ordinating body, which took overall policy decisions. After the coup, it overnight became the top body for not only policy, but also executive decisions. In June 1948 it was considerably enlarged, when the Communist Party fused with the Social Democratic Party. Apart from Social Democrats (Erban E. Fierlinger), Gottwald added to it 'experts' to help him to reshape Czechoslovakia. Nosek was back; Kopřiva in charge of security; Švermová as secretary; Frank another secretary;

Ďuriš and Široký (as Slovaks). In May 1949, the Ninth Congress enlarged it still further by adding two secretaries (G. Bareš, V. David) and trade unionists (Krosnář; G. Kliment). It became unwieldy. So, Gottwald, in the name of efficiency and probably on Stalin's suggestion, assumed all the powers of decision as chairman of the presidium. He no longer needed a 'representative' party body, but an 'efficient' one. He had his son-in-law, Dr. Čepička, co-opted and together with Zápotocký they took all the necessary decisions among them. The presidium was no longer convened and soon was engulfed in a bloody purge. The purged members were replaced by nonentities (Novotný, John, Barák). Zápotocký, as Prime Minister, invariably endorsed Gottwald's decisions; in his devotion to the great leader, he even took the unsuspecting Slánský to his doom. Čepička became Gottwald's troubleshooter at home and in the Cominform.

Since the newly established departments of the central committees were supposed to serve the presidium, Gottwald at first made use of them as intelligence gathering agencies. Since he had purged the secretariat, departments deprived of top men had to go for decisions to him. The departments encompassed absolutely everything: the cadre department was responsible for the selection of Communist leaders and Gottwald put in charge L. Kopřiva (Švermová was removed in 1949). This was not power sharing. He supervised Kopřiva in all three jobs he had given him. In the presidium, where he could give instructions; as President he checked on Kopřiva in the Ministry for Security and as party chairman on his work as head of the cadre department. This system of checks was watertight and Kopřiva's statement in 1968 that he was nothing but a messenger boy of his leader rang true. He also claimed that he had stopped work, when the errands became too dangerous.

In addition to the ministry of security Gottwald had a security department at his disposal, finally abolished in 1989. At first the department had little to do, for security problems were dealt with by Soviet experts. Until 1951, the department was headed by J. Šváb, a brother of M. Švermová (secretary of the central committee). She was the widow of Jan Šverma, Gottwald's companion during the war. She was determined to build for herself and her family a cozy niche in the party's apparat. However, security work was risky. Soon Švermová's downfall was followed by Šváb's liquidation. The department was taken over by J. Šalga, a singularly grey apparatchik, who survived as head the years of Gottwald's cult, but failed to make a political career out of the assignment. This was rather untypical, for even his deputies (O. Papež, K. Innemann and others) prospered as a result. Another head, J. Mamula, survived even the cataclyctic 1968 without arrest. Subsequently he became First Regional Secretary and central committee member. Evidently this department, ostensibly dealing with army and security matters, was not as powerful as had been thought. Security matters were sorted out elsewhere, and the department was used, especially after Gottwald's death, as a screening and interrogation centre.

All the other departments, and their numbers varied as they were often reorganised, were formed for specific purposes. The propaganda and agitation (sometimes ideological) department and the economic departments were the most important. The former had to communicate party policies to the Czechoslovak people, especially after the coup in 1948. Yet, judging from the purge which struck it in 1949, when G. Bares, was removed as head of this department, Gottwald did not approve of the way the department was 'selling' his policies. After Gottwald's death, the department recovered somewhat and was headed by V. Slavík, who became a central committee secretary and reformist in 1968. However, the Czechoslovak Communist Party was not successful with this important department whose heads (Z. Urban, M. Hladík, P. Aueršperg, F. Havlíček, J. Kozel, L. Novotný and V. Bejda) proved to be as ineffective as the policies they propagated. Thus, Hladík gave up party propaganda to become Czechoslovakia's Security Chief, while Kozel disappeared altogether after the purge in 1969.

The economic department was to supervise and co-ordinate the Czechoslovak economy. But it soon proved unequal to this task. Most of its heads literally rolled (Frejka was executed) as Czechoslovakia's economic performance declined. Only in the 1960s was this department used as a springboard for economic and political careers: L. Adamec rose to become Deputy Premier of the Czech Republic in charge of economy and later Federal Premier; R. Rohlíček, after serving as Federal Minister of Finance, became Deputy Federal Premier and permanent representative with COMECON, while L. Šupka another federal minister was put in charge of technology and investments. J. Baryl even became secretary of the central committee, which was considered the ultimate goal of a departmental apparatchik.

It is obvious that, in the communist system, these departments (and they covered the whole of national life—chemical industry, education, science and health; youth and mass organisation; energy and fuel; industry, transport, services; etc.) were substitutes for governmental departments. After Gottwald's death, President Zápotocký tried to revive the traditional Czechoslovak political institutions without destroying those of Gottwald and failed. President Novotný hoped to rid himself gradually of Gottwald's apparat because it 'needed terror to work', and he disliked terror. It was argued later that, since Novotný insisted on retaining the power of the presidency and remaining the party leader, he could not possibly rid himself of the Gottwald system. Still, he was prepared to permit his government to carry out the policies he had approved in any way it thought fit. He also allowed a greater say in policy formulation to the central committee and the government. But he retained tight control over central committee departments and the secretariat. These contradictions resulted in economic failures and they in turn brought about the downfall of Novotný's system.

5

PRAGUE SPRING 1968

After Stalin's death in 1953, every Communist Party in Eastern Europe passed through a crisis: those in Poland and Hungary were particularly acute and the Communist regimes were badly shaken by them. A notable exception seemed to be Czechoslovakia, where the Stalinist leadership survived the 20th Congress of the Soviet Party, and the subsequent de-Stalinisation; President Novotný was toppled from power only in 1968.

Antonin Novotný did not succeed Gottwald directly, but after four years of intermediary Presidency of A. Zápotocký. Prior to 1957, he had led the party and, after Zápotocký's death, held both offices like Gottwald before him. Though he was an experienced apparatchik steeped in totalitarian methods, he had two basic weaknesses. He did not know much about the Czechoslovak state in particular, and politics in general. Above all, he was a simple man with simple solutions. Thus, for example, he knew nothing about the Slovak problem and thought it could be solved by having the troublesome Slovaks arrested. He was equally ignorant of the interplay of forces in politics, and considered his faction as his property and others as his enemies. He had no idea why the economy was performing so badly, and thought of purging managers to improve it. Despite these weaknesses, he possessed a quiet self-assurance: he had survived the troubles of 1953 and 1956, lived through a series of economic crises in the early 1960s and successfully fought off several intra-party bids to get rid of him. Why should he not survive twenty more years. In his 25 years in power he had a minister of the Interior, R. Barák, and his 'group' arrested, tried and sentenced to fifteen years in goal. Široký and others were dismissed, declared responsible for the bloody purges within the party, and he still went on as President-leader. Unfortunately, for him, the factors that were at play now were more difficult to identify and deal with. Thus, he was quite unaware of the dangers facing him in December 1967.

In a sense, Novotný made sure of his downfall the moment he was compelled to head de-Stalinisation, after 1956. One by one, though extremely slowly, his political companions were dismissed. In 1963, the tough Premier, V. Široký, was retired and the 'soft' J. Lenárt, also a Slovak, replaced him. To Novotný's surprise, Lenárt proved as pliant as his predecessor, only slightly more reluctant to carry out Novotný's simple orders. In the early 1960s, many purged Czech communists were rehabilitated, and after 1964 the Slovaks, too. Many resumed party office and some became members of Lenárt's government. Nonetheless, at the 13th Communist Party Congress, in June 1966, Novotný felt at home, among his old companions of terror days. No changes were noticeable: O. Černík replaced another old-timer, Fierlinger, in the party presidium. However, 13% new members of the central committee joined that body, among them the recently rehabilitated ones. Outside the congress, within the Communist Party itself, more radical changes were occurring, but Novotný did not know of them.

After the 13th Congress, he settled down to what was for him the routine of governing the country. He wanted to continue his slow thaw and pounce resolutely on troublemakers, as he used to in the past. However, the introduction of a new economic system, which he did not understand and which provoked the suicide of many a good communist manager, disturbed him. The recently elected Central Committee was restless, seeing his ignorance. He had no idea what should be done, and instead of searching for solutions with his friends, he antagonised them. According to his best friend, secretary J. Hendrych, "the first secretary hardly ever met the Communist leaders collectively, but instead one at a time and then made all decisions alone".

Unknown to Novotný, three loose factions existed within the central committee and the Party. The one consisted of party economists and was headed by O. Černík and Professor O. Šik. Černík was a member of the presidium, head of the Planning Commission: he knew full well of the precarious state of the Czechoslovak economy. It was he who succeeded in persuading the presidium to endorse the 'new' economic system. However, he and his fellow technocrats reached the conclusion that a change in economics had to be matched by political changes, otherwise it would not work either. Professor Šik was the author of the new system; he and his economic experts, were politically unimportant, but were putting pressure on the leadership to give them a freer hand in implementing reforms. The 'faction' was not organised: their discontent with Novotný's leadership was the only link among them.

The latent discontent of Slovak Communists with Prague centralism, now reinforced by the rehabilitated victims of the personality cult, was responsible for emergence of a Slovak faction. Though the Slovaks had real grievances against the Czech domination of the state, they could hardly voice them publicly. Since 1918, their dissatisfaction invariably smacked of high treason: they could be accused of 'nationalist separatism', leading to the destruction of Czechoslovakia. In the recent past, it meant arrest and prison. Their only hope was a change in the party leadership. But even then, it was not certain that an equitable solution to their problems would be found. Passive because of the past experience, the Slovaks had been waiting patiently for seventy years for such a chance.

The third group was only a loose collection of younger Communist leaders who were rising in the party hierarchy, were critical of the old generation and despised their 'antiquated methods'. These young men in a hurry had recently reached posts of significant influence. They were appalled by the primitive minds and manners of the old guard. The most experienced among them was D. Kolder, who had joined the presidium in 1962, followed by a young Slovak, A. Dubček, in 1963. It should be added that this 'generation group' cut across boundaries and many 'economists' belonged to it. Several of the key apparatchiks, such as the regional secretaries in Moravia, Dr. Špaček and Ing. Voleník, as well as the Slovak secretary, V. Bilak, were members of it. Despite the existence of these loose national pressure groups, Novotny could have stayed in power, had he maintained the unity of his own faction.

In 1967, two events shook the old guard. The first was the Writers' Congress in June 1967. The presidium member, J. Hendrych, could not cope at the congress with the writers complaints and criticism and resorted to threats and bullying. The most vociferous writers were expelled from the party, the writers' union journal was suppressed and even a show trial was staged with a young writer, J. Beneš, sentenced to five years imprisonment. Before the leaders had time to recover from the congress, Prague students voiced legitimate grievances in a street riot. They were roughly repressed. The students had always been a headache for the older leaders. Even when the party allowed them to let steam off at the traditional Majales (May celebrations), they invariably caused public disturbances. However, in November 1967, the repression of students by police brutality was symbolic. In the same month in 1939, the Germans had repressed a similar demonstration as roughly as the communist police. Indignation was widespread, but unlike in 1989, the student trouble was exploited by the party to rid itself of the Novotný leadership.

In September 1967, after several border incidents, the tough border-guards, a communist elite force, fired at and killed escapees. Novotný seized on these examples of toughness to intimidate his opponents, but instead frightened his own faction. They thought he wanted to launch another purge. To this confusion the Slovaks added their own: they asked publicly for new constitutional arrangements within the Czechoslovak Republic. In October 1967, Novotný used these demands to attack openly A. Dubček, a presidium member and first secretary of the Slovak Communist Party. He accused him of nationalism-separatism. All the Slovaks were indignant at this unfounded accusation. Only M. Chudík, the chairman of the Slovak National Council and presidium member, supported Novotný. However, the Prime Minister, J. Lenárt, rejected Novotný's allegations, as did many others. Now the Slovaks closed their ranks against the Novotný faction, and waited for a pretext to deal it a deathblow.

Novotný wanted to sort out outstanding problems at the December session of the Central Committee. A week before the meeting, he invited the Soviet first secretary, L. Brezhnev, to Prague, to explain himself and strengthen his position vis-à-vis his party opponents. Inexplicably he allowed Brezhnev to see other presidium members and the 'accused' Slovaks as well. Dubček who had grown up in the Soviet Union and spoke perfect Russian, was able to persuade Brezhnev that he was neither a Slovak 'nationalist' nor a 'separatist'. He also obtained from Brezhnev a pledge of neutrality: the Czechs and the Slovaks would sort out their problems, without Soviet interference. Thus, instead of strengthening his hand, Novotný made certain of his downfall.

On 19 December 1967, the party presidium met to deal with the current political situation and to prepare the agenda and resolutions for the meeting. Novotný and his group failed to put forward any constructive proposals concerning the economy and the Slovak prob-lem. Their clumsiness forced together a coalition of Czech 'economists' (Černík, Kolder) and Slovak 'nationalists' (Dubček). Two of Novotný's friends, J. Dolanský and J. Hendrych, suddenly and unexpectedly switched sides and the presidium was deadlocked. While Novotný, supported by Lenárt, Chudík, Šimůnek and Lastovička could paralyse the proceedings, they could no longer have their decisions approved. The deadlock in the presidium had to be resolved by the Central Committee. However, the debate at the meeting went against Novotný, who, therefore, tried to adjourn the meeting over the Christmas holiday before a vote could be taken. A leadership crisis was on whether Novotný wanted it or not.

Curiously the crisis reached its climax during the Christmas recess. Novotný tried to postpone the resumption of the meeting as long as possible, and only reluctantly gave in to Kolder's ultimatum. During the recess Černík and his allies heard of rumours that the President's security man, Mamula, had prepared lists of persons to be arrested—the list apparently included Černík, Dubček, and altogether some 1000 Communist 'radicals'. The President was also said to be ready to use the army against the central committee, if it voted his ouster. The rumours were probably false, but convinced still hesitant members that President Novotný, whose political past was questionable, would 'liquidate' them. Even before adjourning, the plenary session elected a preparatory commission to make its recommendations to the resumed meeting. The preparatory commission now voted by 9 to 3 to recommend to the central committee the dismissal of the first secretary.

On 5 January 1968, the central committee resumed its plenary session and Novotný himself announced his resignation as first secretary. He remained President and proposed J. Lenárt as his successor. But this desperate manoeuvre of his was defeated. The opposition factions had struck a bargain by which the lonely Slovak outsider, Dubček, succeeded Novotný. To balance the power within the presidium in favour of the 'victorious' faction, four new members were added (Špaček, Borůvka, Rigo, a Slovak gypsy and Piller another Czech economist). Nonetheless Dubček's position in the presidium remained precarious for some time. Bohemia's capital, Prague and five other regions were solidly under the control of Novotný's friends. Dubček's own Slovakia was hopelessly divided: one region was pro-Novotný (Cvik), Bratislava and the eastern region pro-Dubček; the western region neutral. The new presidium member, Špaček, brought with him two Moravian regions (southern and northern), but the northern, formerly Kolder's fief, appeared undecided.

To take over the party machine the new first secretary had no choice but to widen the coup de palais and launch a 'revolution' from above. While the Slovak Central Committee met and resolutely purged the pro-Novotný elements, the Czechs proved much tougher. M. Chudík tried to resign, but was ignominiously dismissed. R. Cvik, was also removed and Slovakia submitted to the new leadership. However, Moravia's quiet adhesion to the new leadership did not solve the crisis either. The two historical lands represented a small part of the machine, if compared to Bohemia and the capital, Prague,

Novotný's powerbase.

There and then, Dubček decided to take the gamble of appealing to public opinion to resolve a party problem. When, late in January 1968, Czech journalists came to him for the customary guidance and instructions, he told them that they would no longer be guided, but left free to voice their own opinions and interpretations. This announcement of freedom of the press (communication media in fact) launched a more fundamental purge than was usual in a Communist country.

In January 1968, it was clear that whatever came in the wake of freedom of the communication media would harm Novotný more than Dubček. The victorious radicals were confident that they could control the unleashed force and use it in the narrow party sense. They reasoned that, since they came to the Central Committee meeting without a plan, were only vaguely linked together and nonetheless had defeated Novotný and his faction, they could handle the communication media. Not only could journalists write freely, but banned journals reappeared to strengthen the criticism of the communist past. Novotný was discredited and made responsible for all existing wrongs. Then suddenly the writers' journal, *Literární Listy*, and other newspapers launched a wider liberalisation campaign, outside the limits of Dubček's intentions. J. Pelikán, head of the television network, quickly jumped on the bandwagon, while J. Smrkovský and O. Šik agitated Prague citizens at public meetings in this sense. The floodgates of criticism were opened. Novotný and his faction emerged as bloodthirsty tyrants, responsible for all the past 'deformations'. In consequence, a wave of panic struck the communists.

On 5 March 1968, it became known that one of the most corrupt and ruthless of Novotný's creatures, Major-General Šejna, had escaped from Czechoslovakia and defected to the United States. Marshal Yakubovsky had to pay a special visit to Prague to find out the extent of Šejna's betrayal. As far as the Soviets were concerned, this defection sealed the fate of the Novotný faction. Dubček and his friends could purge Bohemia in the usual Communist way without arousing Russian wrath: throughout March 1968, suicides (General Janko, Dr. Brežanský), dismissals and resignations followed each other. Mamula, formerly in charge of the security department, had the audacity to call the panic White terror. In fact this was an example of what free public opinion could do to totalitarian structures.

Throughout January–April 1968, Novotný and his faction held on to their posts. On the other hand, the new leadership was split: Dubček led now a centrist group, concerned more with the party, while Šik and Smrkovský the radicals wanted more general reforms. However, to oust the Novotnýites and appease public opinion, Dubček decided to draw up a new action programme for the party and launch the judicial rehabilitation of all the victims of communist terror. These measures were intended to give the party a human face after it had been tarnished by the Novotnýites, and justify its holding on to power. However, to outbid the radicals, Dubček appealled, not only to party members, to become involved in this humanisation of communism, but thanks to freedom of expression, to all the citizens. Overnight, meetings raised demands, going clearly beyond Dubček's intentions: thus, workers wanted increased wages, and better managers: intellectuals asked for the freedom to travel abroad: others for free elections. Some gatherings dared to suggest the creation of an entirely new political system, fully pledged democracy. Many of these proposals were incorporated in the draft programme, but, unlike in 1989, the leading role of the party and marxism-leninism as ideology were left untouched. While these public discussions increased confusion in the country, the rehabilitation campaign finally discredited Novotný and his friends. It was certain they would disappear from public life.

Under pressure from public opinion, Novotný resigned as President before the April plenary session of the central committee. After a spate of regional and district party conferences, many of his friends were dismissed in the provinces. *Rudé Právo*, the party newspaper, abruptly changed sides on 13 March and the whole of the public communications system came firmly on the reformers' side. Dubček himself made several radical speeches, in which he promised everybody something: the Slovaks were promised a real federation and all that it implied (additional jobs in the central government, separate football teams, local autonomy); the Czechs were offered a free press, free speech, assembly and association. In fact everyone could find something to please him among these promises. But, first of all, Dubček had to win the struggle for the party. He convened the plenary session for 3 April 1968. A new presidium had to be elected, for Novotný also resigned from it: J. Smrkovský took his place. Hendrych, Dolanský, Laštovička and Šimůnek also resigned. Their places were taken by Slovaks and Prague centrists; only Lenárt survived, though as a candidate member.

The composition of the new presidium indicated that, while the radicals had achieved the dismissals of conservative leaders, they were a minority in the presidium (Smrkovský, Špaček and Kriegel). Moreover, they lost Borůvka, who was appointed minister of agriculture, and Professor Šik was not elected at all. O. Švestka, editor of the party newspaper, *Rudé Právo*, was a well-known conservative as well as the three candidate members, Lenárt, Kapek and M. Vaculík. The new leadership was a coalition. The same was true of the secretariat: J. Lenárt and Z. Mlynář, cancelled each other out. The new secretary, S. Sádovský, was Dubček's man. If the plenum was not a victory for the radicals, their ideas won widespread support. Novotný himself, who was allowed to speak, claimed credit for them; he had prepared the current 'democratisation' process. The central committee approved the action programme, which though vague, contained many concrete points: secret intra-party elections, right to a passport, a strict division of the executive and legislative power, secret elections with several candidates etc.

Lenárt's government resigned and a new one was formed by O. Černík, which was to implement the party action programme. The old 'satellite' parties, the Socialist (Liberal) Party and the People's (Catholic) Party, were treated with the same contempt as previously and given the old resorts, Ministry of Justice and Health. All else was retained by the Communist Party; radical changes did not apply to the executive. Only the minister of the Interior was a victim of terror years. Professor Šik was held in check by Dr. Štrougal, former Minister of the Interior under Novotný, an economic overlord.

All the party and government changes indicated that a delicate balance of power was attempted by the centrists. The radical elements were allowed in, to counter-balance the old guard. Immediately afterwards, Dubček came under new pressures from the conservatives, who tried a comeback. Many were re-elected at the hastily convened district and regional conferences and one, Žourek, threatened Dubček with the workers' militia. M. Vaculík, who ostensibly had changed sides, was re-elected in Prague. To resist the conservatives, the radicals revived discussions about an officially recognised opposition party and public opinion took up the proposal with enthusiasm. But Dubček ignored it. It became clear that the conservatives could only be eliminated by an extraordinary congress, which would also approve the new programme. Dubček, however, hesitated. After all, Czechoslovakia was still a member of the Warsaw Pact and real democratisation would be interpreted by other communists "as a retreat from Communism". In consequence, he feared either Soviet or Warsaw Pact intervention.

However, in the general excitement, public opinion and communication media were gaining the upper hand. With the return to democracy went the prospect of Western loans. Sooner or later, Dubček and the centrists had to make their choices, if political and above all economic stability were to return.

At this stage, no one even thought of solutions imposed from outside, albeit the Communist allies, specially the USSR, had tried to influence Dubček, from the very beginning of the crisis, in 1967. On 23 March 1968, Dubček was called to Dresden to account for himself: he told the five Warsaw Pact allies (Romania did not attend) that the Communist Party had everything under control, with the exception of the communications media. But he was not afraid of their freedom. A week later, Army General Ludvík Svoboda, a lonely survivor of the post-war era, was elected President and on 18 April 1968, Josef Smrkovský was elected Speaker of the National Assembly. Later, in May 1968, the 'unrepresentative' central committee expelled from the party Bacílek, David, Kohler, Rais and Široký, suspended Novotný's membership and finally convoked the extra-ordinary congress for 9 September 1968. Shortly afterwards, *Literární listy* published an appeal, 2,000 words, signed even by some members of the central committee, asking for more rapid purges of Stalinists still in public life. Although the appeal received its share of publicity, it was not a particularly violent document; however, the Warsaw Pact allies seized on it and determined to use it to wrest concessions from the new leadership: public opinion had to be controlled; anarchy had to stop. Dubček, now under Soviet pressure, repudiated it. At the same time, to demonstrate his independence, he refused to attend the Warsaw Pact meeting scheduled for 14 July 1968.

It now is known that at the Warsaw meeting, (without Romania's participation) the fate of Dubček's Czechoslovakia was sealed. He would either return to orthodox communism, or his Allies would force him to. No action was taken immediately, but the Warsaw Pact command asked for and received permission to send its armies to Czechoslovakia for training purposes. However, their presence failed to intimidate Czechoslovak public opinion. Late in July 1968, the Czechoslovak and Soviet politbyra met at Čierná nad Tisou to negotiate a final compromise agreement. It was made public at Bratislava in the presence of all the Eastern European Communist leaders: Dubček promised to restore some sort of control over communist media. However, three weeks later, when he apparently had failed to keep his promise, Czechoslovakia was suddenly invaded and occupied by the Warsaw Pact armies.

Up to 21 August 1968, on the day of invasion, the problem was whether the Communist Party should remain in power in the Stalinist sense, against the will of a majority of the Czech and Slovak people, or with its consent. Soviet intervention transformed this problem into which party should rule: Dubček's or some one else's, on Soviet terms. Dubček and the new leaders, with the exception of President Svoboda, were arrested and taken to the USSR. A. Indra, who was to proclaim himself Premier, did not dare to. V. Bilak went round Prague in fear for his life. Only G. Husák began to show signs of willingness to come to a compromise with the occupiers. Invasion and occupation seemed to solve nothing, making the Czechoslovak situation only more complex.

On the very eve of the Soviet intervention, the presidium, as could be expected, was disunited. On hearing of the invasion, the declaration condemning it was, nonetheless, approved by seven to four votes (Švestka, Indra, Kolder and Bil'ak). Henceforth the four dissenters went their way and later became enthusiastic 'normalisers'. The invasion itself united the party and the nations behind Dubček, Svoboda, Smrkovský and Černík. Nationalist resistance against foreign invaders, combined with a sense of outrage at foreign parties interfering in the internal affairs of the Czechoslovak party, made the situation rather explosive. (In 1989, the Soviets and their allies proclaimed the invasion a political mistake and apologised.) However, despite this newly found national unity, Czechoslovak resistance remained passive. In the confusion caused by the arrest and deportation of the communist leaders, the Prague city committee decided to proceed with the convocation of the scheduled congress. By 23 August, the extraordinary congress eliminated all the Stalinists, as well as 'collaborators', from the party, with seven exceptions. The presidium consisted of all the reformers who had become prominent after Novotný's fall: A. Dubček, J. Smrkovský, O. Černík, J. Spaček, F. Kriegel, B. Šimon, Č. Císař, O. Šik, V. Šilhan, O. Slavík, L. Hrdinová, V. Matějíček, B. Kabrna, and 14 others, among whom Gustáv Husák. However, within a fortnight, after the signature of the Moscow Diktat, the 'underground' congress was annulled and Dubček restored many 'collaborators' by co-option: V. Bil'ak, E. Erban, were back in the presidium, others in the central committee. Dubček, Svoboda and Smrkovský were allowed to return from Moscow on these terms: they had to take back the 'collaborators' and start again on their reforms, as if the invasion had not taken place. The Red Army would remain in the country, to make sure that reforms did not get out of hand.

Though the crisis within the Communist Party and the country lasted over a year, two more years had to be spent on 'stabilisation' or 'normalisation', as it was called. In fact, the results of the reform year 1968 were one by one abolished, and one more principle added to the cannon of orthodoxy, proletarian internationalism. Henceforth, all the East European countries put it in their constitutions: Soviet intervention was automatic, if communism was in danger of collapsing. Curiously Dubček's reforms, if implemented, would have led to the re-establishment of the pre-1948 system, with its political freedom and mixed economy. This was Gottwald's ideal of the "Czechoslovak way to socialism", before Stalin put a stop to it. Now Brezhnev was blocking Dubček's "socialism with a human face". Throughout 1968, these ideas had galvanised the Czech and Slovak nations, and despite Soviet occupation continued to be expressed the only way the people knew: concrete bills were put before, discussed by and then passed by the Czechoslovak National Assembly (Parliament) as laws of the country.

The National Assembly, which on 1 January 1969 had become the Federal Assembly, was composed of unrepresentative deputies elected in 1964 (the scheduled election in 1968 was to be based on a new electoral law). Nonetheless, its majority seemed to have remembered the busy pre-February 1948 days, with their techniques of parliamentary business, committee meetings, loud plenary debates, and acted accordingly. While in the period 1964–68 the Assembly met on average in two plenary sessions a year, during 1968 it held twelve plenary session, some lasting several days. Thus, the January plenary session approved the budget; in February the law making Bratislava the capital of Slovakia was passed. In two sessions in March the Assembly elected a new President, Ludvík Svoboda, in April a new Speaker (J. Smrkovský) and a new presidium. During the same month, the government's programme was discussed and in May a vote of confidence was given to Premier O. Černík. In June, a great number of laws were passed: Czechoslovakia became a federal state; the rehabilitation bill was made a law together with a new press law; the membership of the new Czech National Council was fixed; the Central People's Control Commission was transformed into a parliamentary investigating committee; work was begun on a new Constitution and the government's measures were checked and endorsed. On 1 July, the Assembly elected the new Czech Council and then adjourned for the summer holidays. The committees continued their work throughout the summer, even during the invasion by the Warsaw Pact armies. Shortly before the invasion, the 26th plenary session was convoked and, though it was interrupted, it passed a whole series of laws governing the federation in September 1968; a new law on the National Front was also passed. In October, the plenary session passed a law governing the presence of the Soviet armies in Czechoslovakia, as well as the final Federation law, requiring amendments to the Constitution. Although many laws were not passed (e.g. a new electoral law) the extraordinary level of legislative activity of the 'rump' parliament achieved more than all the parliaments since 1948. This new political dynamism was detectable also in the economic sphere in which much less could be done by legislation. Despite the disruption caused by the invasion, the economy had progressed and corrected the lag of the previous five years. It was the leaders who gradually became tired and gave up the fight. One by one, Dubček's friends and allies either resigned or were dismissed. In April 1969, when most of the reformers had been eliminated, the Soviets dared to get rid of Dubček himself. Under the pretext of an anti-Soviet riot in Prague, following a victory by ČSSR over the USSR in ice hockey, he was forced to resign. His successor was another Slovak, G. Husák, a 'realist' and champion of compromises with the Soviets. Almost immediately, the new first secretary launched a massive party purge (150,000) and had all the reforms modified or repealed by the Federal Assembly. A new government headed by L. Štrougal completed his takeover. By 1971 Husák felt strong enough to have himself re-elected as first secretary by a normalised party congress.

6

HUSÁK'S RISE AND FALL

It took the cynical opportunist Husák eighteen months finally to condemn and reverse the 1968 reforms. In December 1970, the Central Committee, at his bidding and despite his promises, approved "The Lessons of the Crisis Development". The lessons meant a return to orthodoxy: Socialist democracy based on democratic centralism, collective ownership of means of production, Socialist legality, the leading role of the Communist Party, the economy regulated by state plan. Husák put Štrougal in charge of government and economy, Indra of the Legislative organs and Bil'ak and Lenárt of the party, with ailing Svoboda as the only survivor.

Many laws were revoked immediately: the National Front Act, the Press Act; many were simply not enforced and the Rehabilitation Act amended. The most fundamental law, the Federation Act, remained in force as if to prove that Husák was retaining all the sound ideas of 1968. However, in 1989, when they could, the Slovaks again accused him of discrimination, and non-application of this act. The sad, Soviet viceroy in fact reversed all progress in Czechoslovakia, to prove his loyalty to his Soviet master. Thus, even the mildly liberal electoral law of 1967 was discarded; in security matters he went back to Gottwald whose victim he once was. In 1975, he felt less insecure after taking over the presidency, but it was obvious that he had failed to take over even the purged party.

To control the party more or less securely, Husák had to purge it severely: he had to eliminate not only his old opponents, the Novotnýites, but also his erstwhile friends and allies of 1968. In severity Husák's purge could be compared with Gottwald's in 1948–49, when the 'democratic' political party was transformed into an instrument of totalitarianism. The central apparat of the party was strengthened and Husák appointed as heads of central committee departments handpicked Slovaks, making them at the same time members of the central committee: his private secretary, M. Beňo, entering the central committee in 1976; V. Bejda in charge of propaganda and agitation; while M. Kudzej and, after his death, A. Turzo were controlling military and security matters; another Slovak, J. Varga, was put in charge of agriculture. However, Husák's domination of the party was even more complete than this organisation control illustrates: all genuine political leaders had been dismissed as a result of the upheaval in 1968 and Husák was really the lonely survivor.

From 1 January 1969, when Czechoslovakia became a federal republic, new federal institutions came into being, thus enabling Husák to rid himself of potential rivals in the party; however, it was only in 1971 that Indra was kicked upstairs, to become the Federal Speaker, while Štrougal became Premier in 1970. After a period of fluidity, Korčák and Colotka became Premiers of the Czech and Slovak republics respectively, and remained in the party presidium *ex officio*, both being 'technocrats' rather than party leaders. Although the top posts in the Federal government, and in Czech and Slovak governments, were reserved for party politicians, the stress was nevertheless on their technocratic ability: only M. Lúčan, Federal Deputy Premier, seems to have been a straightforward party hack. The other Deputy Premiers had either administrative or technocratic backgrounds, F. Hamouz, V. Hůla, R. Rohlíček and Šimon. The purely technocratic Deputy Premiers, K. Laco, J. Gregor, J. Zahradník were there on their administrative merit, as was the case with the majority of ministers, with the exception of the Minister of the Interior and Foreign Affairs, who had to be politicians and were Dr. Husák's choice. Army General Dzúr was another lonely survivor of the 1968, and, despite being a Slovak, his power declined. The Federal government did not contain any representatives of the other political parties, which was not the case in pre-1968 days.

The re-organization of Parliament also enabled Husák to appoint there the most pro-Soviet and compromised Novotnýites. The Federal Assembly now consists of two chambers: the People's Chamber and the Nation's Chamber. In addition, each republic has its own legislative chamber, the Czech and Slovak National Council. J. Smrkovský, the National Assembly Speaker, did not become the Federal Speaker, only the chairman of the People's Chamber. The Slovak, Dr. Hanes, was the Federal Speaker (with a short interruption in 1969, when P. Colotka and Dubček occupied that position for several months). In 1971, after an election, A Indra became Speaker; Hanes was shamefully relegated to the chairmanship of the Nation's Chamber succeeding another Slovak, V. Mihalík, J. Marko, until then Foreign Minister, became the first Deputy Speaker, while V. David, Gottwald's and Novotný's Foreign Minister became chairman of the People's Chamber. The National Councils were chaired by E. Erban and O. Klokoč, the least controversial of the 1968 men. Husák rid himself of all the surviving Stalinists in the Federal Parliament: E. Laštovička, still very active; V. Nový, much less; O. Voleník, drinking himself ill, while another inebriated Stalinist J. Trojan, killed himself in a car accident.

After the November 1971 election, the composition of the Federal Assembly became as arbitrary and contemptuous of the non-Communist parties as under Novotný: while in the Nation's Chamber the Communist Party had 102 seats, the Czech Socialists had 7, the Czech People's Party 8, and the 2 Slovak parties had 2 each. Paradoxically the non-party deputies increased their own representation to 29. In the People's Chamber, the Communists had 143 seats; Czech Socialists 13, the People's Party 8 seats and the 2 Slovak parties 2 each. Here again the non-party members did well controlling 32 seats.

However, the Federal Assembly, after its wide purge in the years 1969–71, lost its significance and became again similar to the Supreme Soviet. In 1974, Václav David, Chairman of the People's Chamber, in which federal legislation should be thrashed out and prepared, reported on its activity in the terms of the 14th Communist Party Congress' instructions and central committee resolutions. He called for improved cooperation with the Slovak and Czech Councils, either because these Councils were more active or because they intruded into the federal legislation. Certainly there was room for overlap in the bills prepared and the acts passed: Acts on inventions and improvements, bills on scientific development, transport and services and especially on education and youth whose executive ministries the federation did not possess. Even though David claimed that the committee work was the real basis of business transacted by the People's Chamber, only few important acts were passed between 1971–74. Instead the Federal Assembly seems to have concentrated on foreign affairs (it is, of course, its exclusive right) and on training of its own members to conduct the legislative business in committees and plenary sessions. Thus in the legislature, Husák's normalisation had a deadening effect and was, in fact, a return to the 'classical' Gottwald and Novotný days.

It took some time before it became clear how the federal arrangements would work. In 1969, it still looked as if the judiciary would be separated and work according to Act 143 passed in 1968. However, the amendments 125 and 13, passed in 1970 and 1971, respectively, proved that here there would also be a return to past arrangements:

indeed the 15th Congress of the Communist Party proclaimed its undivided supremacy and made the federation merely responsible for the implementation of its decisions and directives. Although the legislative remained primary on paper, all its powers and prerogatives (control, questions) were amended so that the executive was once again able to work without any control, 'according to the socialist division of labour'; the judiciary likewise maintained Socialist legality. The procedural rules of the Federal Assembly were amended in 1970 (Act 20); the President's Chancellory powers were trimmed in 1970 (Act 17); rigid federal planning was legalised in 1970 (Act 145), and the acts governing the judges and procuracy were passed in 1969 (Acts 147, 156, 158) and then amended in 1970 (Acts 20, 19).

In the new federal set up, it was not clear how the most important question of state security was resolved. After its collapse in 1968, the security services were taken over by their Soviet counterparts, and were only gradually re-established. Albeit J. Pavel, Minister of the Interior, was forced to resign immediately after the Soviet invasion, his veteran successor, J. Pelnář, refused to do much about improving state security, whose abuses in the past had been the real causes of Novotný's fall. Dr. Husák had to dismiss Pelnář and appointed his private secretary, R. Kaska as Minister of the Interior, before anything was done. However, already in 1970, the appointment of Major General M. Kosnar heralded a new era for state security. Kosnar was an experienced, Soviet approved security officer, who as a Slovak could perhaps be trusted by Dr. Husák. However, in security matters, Husák had to compromise with Indra, who had his personal secretary, M. Hladík, appointed as top security operative (in Czechoslovak terms). Hladík, lecturer in journalism at Prague University, Doctor of Philosophy, and former head of the central committee's progaganda department, became head of the second department of the Ministry of the Interior. While Hladík safeguarded the security of the Indra faction, the security service seemed to concentrate on propaganda actions, such as isolating Czechoslovakia from foreign 'propaganda' and bullying artists and historians. This security expert, apart from sentencing a handful of fellow party leaders for 'anti-constitutional' activities, obviously left the responsibility for real security matters to his Soviet advisers and operatives, who had installed themselves in Prague in large numbers. Still to use security services for even such limited purposes, the Communist Party insisted on repealing Act 166/1968 in which security matters were more or less concretised, and superseded it with a vacuous Act 128/1970. The Czechoslovak People's Army, responsible for external security was doubly humiliated in the turmoil of 1968: as a result of Major General Šejna's desertion and subsequent appeals of Lieutenant General V. Prchlík for new arrangements in the Warsaw Pact, it was completely isolated within the alliance; however, with its failure to resist the invasion, while it might have saved world peace, it ceased to be an army and to serve its purpose. Both Dubček and Husák tried to resuscitate it (after an extensive and unpublicised purge) by means of a Council for the Defence of the State. This Council made some sense while the President of the Republic and Commander-in-Chief of the armed forces was a general, who was at the same time chairman of the Council, but it ceased to have any meaning after President Svoboda's retirement in 1975. In any case, the Council since its inception in 1969 (Act 10/ 1969) met less and less frequently, until it effaced itself completely on the lines of the Soviet Supreme Defence Council. In 1969, the people's army seems to have temporarily found a new purpose, when it was used in August to supress popular and widespread demonstrations against the Soviet occupation of the country. In 1976, at the 15th Congress, the army was finally compensated for its collapse in 1968, and its humiliations afterwards, by having its representation in the central party organs more than tripled: in addition to the Minister of Defence and the Politruk, the two first deputy ministers as well as a vice-minister and commander of the Western Region were elected. However, the Czechoslovak People's Army still without a defensive purpose, remains an extremely costly instrument of power; if permitted by its allies, Czechoslovakia would very much like to cut the size of this useless instrument.

During the year of reforms, it was stated many times that the independence of the judges and procurators would have to be guaranteed by law. However, in the hectic days of 1968, the National Assembly never found the time to prepare a bill regulating the independence of courts and procuracy. Only in 1969 was Chapter VIII of the 1960 Constitution slightly modified, but the constitutional principles governing the courts and the procuracy were left unchanged. The judges were 'elected', they were 'independent' (without any other specification), while the procurators were in charge of 'Socialist legality'. All these innovations were purely formal, and all that was really changed were the structures in the terms of the federation: the Supreme Court of the Federation and two republican Supreme Courts were added. Local people's courts were abolished and their function was taken over by a single magistrate. The Procuracy was also organised on the federal level and both republics had their republican procuracies. The Federal Assembly finalised these arrangements in 1970, in a series of acts: new procuracy—modification of Act 60/1965 by Acts 147/ 1969 and 20/1970; new courts and judges—modification of Act 36/ 1964 by Acts 156/1969 and 19/1970. Thus, despite new acts, nothing was really reformed in the sector of the judiciary.

'Normalisation' did bring back political stability to Czechoslovakia. However, to achieve this Dr. G. Husák, Secretary General of the Communist Party and President, was forced to return to the previous power principles, if not in the form of the demised Novotný and Gottwald systems: practically nothing was retained of the 1968 reform. All that the Husák system had to show for its arbitrariness and lack of freedom was a qualified economic success. However, even under Gottwald and Novotný, the Czechs used to joke about their lack of aspiration to greater freedom: provided people had 'enough beer, pork and dumplings with sauerkraut; they could not care less about freedom and democracy.

Manchester   1980

CZECHOSLOVAKIA'S VELVET REVOLUTION: NOVEMBER 1989

After the removal of A. Dubček and most of his team from power in April 1969, it took G. Husák almost 18 months before he dared to break his promises and reverse the reforms. At the same time he put a new team in charge of the country: L. Štrougal became Federal Premier, Korčák and Colotka headed the Czech and Slovak governments; A. Indra, Federal Speaker; K. Hoffmann Trade Unions; Bil'ak, Lenárt, Kempný and Kapek held the most important party offices; only Svoboda remained as President, until his retirement in 1975. Then Husák purged the communist party of some 500,000 followers of Dubček. The man who presided this purge was Husák's eventual successor in 1987, M. Jakeš. Though there was some passive resistance to Husák's repressive measures, no one dared to oppose them publicly. Both the surviving leaders and party members quickly came to terms with the changed conditions and cynically helped Husák to "normalise" the country. In return they could take advantage either of their offices in the state or the party apparat to enrich themselves, or remain passive, neglecting party work and burying themselves in their daily tasks. For some twenty years, Husák's power arrangements were an example of communist stability.

Husák considered that in the totalitarian system, as he had set it up, the control of the party was sufficient to keep him in power undisturbed. Nonetheless, as a good lawyer, he added legal measures to re-inforce the system and calm down the population. In 1970, Act 70 stopped all the rehabilitations of persons living abroad. The year before Act 150 had enumerated all the 'political crimes' that a citizen could commit: subvert the republic, damage the the socialist state, incite others against the state, misuse religion, slander the republic and the head of the state, and engage in terrorism. This was a tough law decreed to intimidate the population. Though it was rarely used, Husák did not hesitate to use it to crack down on the intellectual protests of the Chartre 77 movement, or the demonstrations early in 1989.

With political stability thus insured, Husák became head of state, in order to combine the presidency once again with the party office. In 1978, the familiar problems of the national economy re-appeared, but he succeeded in keeping them under control. Unexpectedly, dangers to his long rule arose from abroad rather than at home. The first signs of discomfiture came after a series of Soviet leaders' deaths from 1982–5. With his sponsors dead, Gorbachev, a newly emerged young leader, wanted to divest the Soviet Union of its turbulent past, including the two occupations of Czechoslovakia and Afghanistan. Ten years after the 1975 crisis, the Czechoslovak economy began to falter, albeit its decline was not comparable to those of the other communist bloc countries. In response to Gorbachev, Husák loosened control over public opinion (the local equivalent of glasnost) and permitted foreign travel; as a consequence the Czechs and Slovaks began to realise how economically backward their country was, compared to the West. This realisation, coupled with the coming changes in the direction of the economy, and with the anniversary of the failed Prague spring, suddenly and unexpectedly brought the minor crisis to the boil. With the accession to power by Mikhail Gorbachev, Husák's ruling group found itself in a blind alley, since they owed their power to his predecessors. Gorbachev was known to be hostile towards the intervention in Afghanistan, but also towards the one in Czechoslovakia. With perestroika accompanied by glasnost, Gorbachev's problem with the rulers in Czechoslovakia became public property. In this political confusion, Czechoslovak leaders declared themselves willing to launch their own perestroika and even glasnost, if allowed to remain in power, as early as 1985.

However, the elderly Husák prevaricated, fully aware of his contradictory position. Gorbachev turned to the "younger" men and 'forced' them to take away the party leadership from Husák. Finally, in 1987, Milos Jakeš was elected as secretary general, but practically all the other 'old' men remained in power: Alois Indra, Josef Kempný, Peter Colotka and Husák himself as President. Only the ultra-collaborationist V. Bil'ak was partially retired, to be followed a year later by the reformist L. Štrougal. The renewed team proclaimed its views on domestic perestroika and glasnost, in a solemn statement before the Federal Assembly made by the new Federal Premier, L. Adamec, in November 1988.

Very quickly, it became clear that the old leaders could only vote perestroika resolutions, not implement them: perestroyka was not doing well in Czechoslovakia. With glasnost it was even worse: no one wanted to admit that they were wrong in 1968, when asking for Soviet intervention. Gorbachev, for internal reasons, wanted to make his condemnation of this intervention public. It was difficult to reconcile these contradictory positions. In 1988, Jakeš made an effort to get out of this party political mess. He again purged the most compromised party leaders and brought in a few 'younger' men. L. Adamec, 'elected' to the politbyro this time, became Federal Premier; he had a long experience of government and a reformist penchant. But otherwise the new appointments proved to be provincial aparatchiks, incapable of real reforms. Like the previous reshuffle of the politbyro and the secretariat, sacked hardliners were replaced by hardliners, among them the subsequently infamous M. Štepan and the rising Youth leaders, V. Mohorita.

Throughout 1988–89, Premier Adamec talked of reform, particularly when abroad, but at home the hardliners blocked the execution of the timid reforms that were passed by the politbyro. The ideological dictator, secretary J. Fojtik, also a recent promotion, did not espouse glasnost, but instead threatened with party explusion anybody, who would dare to breach the problem of Soviet intervention in Czechoslovakia in 1968.

The year 1989 started badly for Jakeš's hardline leadership. The team felt relieved to have survived the anniversary year 1988 without great upheavals. But immediately in January 1989, special riot police and paratroopers had to disperse mass demonstrations commemorating the anniversary of Jan Palach, who burnt himself to death in 1969, in protest against Soviet intervention. The dissident playwright, V. Havel, was re-arrested and given another sentence for organising this public disturbance. There had been rioting in May, August and in October as well, but the specially trained anti-riot troops had seemed capable of controlling the situation.

Nonetheless, Gorbachev was far from satisfied with Jakeš's performance as Czechoslovakia's leader, and in July sent him an ultimatum:

either he would admit his error about 1968, re-instate the 160,000 expelled communists and purge all the "collaborators", except himself, or he would lose Gorbachev's support. To save his position, Jakeš promised action by October, but could not keep his promise: his position in the party became shaky; he was busy controlling an explosive situation at home and hardliners threatened him with revolt, if he carried out promises given to Gorbachev. When nothing happened, Fojtík was issued with another ultimatum while on a visit to Moscow: the Soviet condemnation of the 1968 invasion would be published!

By November, unknown to Jakeš, it was too late anyway to do anything about 1968 and its aftermath. With Poland and Hungary free and the neighbouring East German communist regime collapsing he was falsely confident that he and his riot police could control even a Leipzig-type mass demonstration. This false sense of security led him to authorise a commemorative student demonstration on 17 November 1989: fifty years earlier, Prague students had demonstrated against the Nazi occupation, were violently dispersed and one of them died. Immense crowds (some estimate 50,000) gathered and heard official speakers without violence. However, after this 'pious' ceremony in a different part of the city, a large number of students (over 15,000) decided to march to Wenceslas Square to have their own commemoration. It is now said that a secret police agent was responsible for this diversion, in order to provoke a clash between the students and the riot police. The student procession was swelling all the way to the historical centre: people stopping their cars to join in; whole tram loads abandoned their journey to march back with the students.

It is now certain that the politbyro did not want to suppress the demonstration with force. However, Jakeš and Štepan told the police authorities not to allow the students into Wenceslas Square, which was paramount to ordering their dispersal by special riot police before reaching the Square. At the lower end of the square, at Národní třída (National Avenue), the elite troops of communism clashed with unarmed demonstrators, making a short shrift of them. 291 were seriously injured and over 100 arrested. Even as students and passersby tried to flee, they were trapped by the police and brutally beaten. Within two hours, all was quiet in the historical centre of Prague and a short official communiqué said that a small crowd of rioters was peacefully dispersed by the police.

If the communist leadership was prepared to ignore this additional riot in the disturbed year of 1989, the population was not. On 18 November, fantastic rumours circulated in Prague about police brutality and student casualties: most persistent rumours claimed that one student was killed by the police. Ordinary citizens were revolted at this "repetition" of Nazi brutalities by the communist police. Crowds formed spontaneously and everyone marched to Wenceslas Square. This time the police failed to respond with violence, for the crowds were too big. Equally spontaneously, dissidents emerged as the leaders of the crowds, but the communist reaction to the events was hesitant and slow.

While the Prague population was demonstrating in increasing numbers, Jakeš carried on as if nothing had happened. On 19 November, he ordered the People's Militia (communist private army) to "protect" industrial enterprises against the demonstrators, but only increased confusion by this measure. By then the army advised him that it would not be used for a violent suppression of mass demonstrations as in China earlier that year. With the party leadership in disarray, panic spread throughout the apparat. Workers were disturbed by police brutality against their 'children' and threatened Štepan with violence, when he came to address them in the OKD enterprise, once the bastion of communist influence. It became obvious that communist paper condemnations of 'the misused' demonstrations were only exciting the population to greater participation in them and were not bringing about a solution of this unprecedented crisis.

Finally, on 24 November, Jakeš was forced to convene an emergency session of the central committee. After a stormy all night debate, Štrougal and Adamec gained sufficient support to oust the entire politbyro, "responsible for the crisis". Karel Urbánek, an obscure provincial apparatchik, was elected in Jakeš's stead and unknown workers emerged overnight in the top organs of the almighty communist party. Even Adamec, though Premier, was not re-elected. Nonetheless, three hardliners remained: Lenárt, Štepán, Zavadil. However, by now it did not really matter, for power was in the streets, with the crowds and their leaders. This became apparent to everybody two days later. Since the crowds objected to the infamous troika (Lenárt, Štepán, Zavadil) remaining in the politbyro, Urbánek purged them and replaced them with further non-entities.

While Jakeš fretted and vacillated, the demonstrating crowds found their natural leaders: V. Havel, the recently released dissident writer; V. Malý, a dissident priest; M. Kubišová, a dissident singer and plenty of other artists and intellectuals. At one stage Alexander Dubček joined them, but then disappeared preferring to engage in backroom negotiations. The intellectual leaders, inspired probably by the East German development, formed themselves into a Civic Forum, thus legitimising their power takeover. Moreover, they launched a nation-wide formation of civic fora, to take over power from the communists all over the country. Unwittingly they copied communist tactics of the 1948 coup and panic struck in turn the allmighty apparat and the party as a whole. Action fora forced communist resignations everywhere; they had their replacement candidates ready. After Prague, other cities joined in mass demonstrations, always led by university students, to express their indignation at the Prague happenings. Civic fora went hand in hand with the spread of these demonstrations, until even the army was subjected to them.

Conscious of the loss of power and rather in panic the new communist leadership tried to resolve the crisis with words: it proclaimed itself a democratic party which would compete in a free election with other parties for power. However, from a proclamation to actual implementation there was still a long way. Premier Adamec began to negotiate with the Central Forum in order to give it power in a coalition government. On 3 December, he headed a government which still had a communist majority. The forum and the students put pressure on him by continuing their demonstrations and as a protest another general strike was proclaimed. Only the threat of a strike forced Adamec's resignation. By 11 December M. Čalfa, a reform communist expert was Premier and his government had a non-communist majority. Subsequently, the communist dominated parliament, Federal Assembly, amended the constitution cancelling the article guaranteeing the communist party's predominant role and another concerning its ideology, marxism-leninism. After the constitutional amendments were passed, they were immediately implemented on all levels of national life. President Husák resigned, and on 29 December V. Havel was elected by the Federal Assembly, still artificially controlled by the communists, unanimously as his successor as had been the case with Husák. Subsequently Dubček became Federal Speaker, dismissed most of the communist deputies, replacing them with coopted ones. Premier Čalfa and two of his deputies left the party and in the end the federal government had only four communists in its midst.

The young men's revolt which had turned into a popular revolution was complete, without any shedding of blood. Gradually, the Civic Forum took over power, dominating not only the Federal government and assembly, but also the national Czech and Slovak governments and councils. The secret police was dissolved and reformed, the freedom of public demonstrations re-asserted; the freedom of press and public expression-media re-established. Economic and political reforms were announced; all sorts of émigrés were invited back to the country. 8–9 June 1990 was fixed as the date for a free general election, by which time the improvised democratic system would give way to a really democratic one: within two years a new democratic constitution would come into force.

For Czechoslovakia it means that the wheel of history has been turned back to the first republican system (1918–38) rather than to the second (1945–48) as forty four parties registered for the election. In the forty one years in power, communism proved itself a bankrupt ideology and as a political system unsuitable for Czechoslovakia. Only the election results will determine who will yield power in Czechoslovakia for the rest of this century. If the communist run election poll is anything to go by, the communist party will gain up to 16% of the vote, not a bad performance for a political party, which has caused a steady national decline in the past forty years of its dictatorship. It is a historical paradox, hard to explain, that the communist system disintegrated under the impact of the same forces that brought it to power in 1948, namely street demonstrations. Husák's fall proves that totalitarian systems are as fragile as liberal democracies to internal 'subversion', if effected by the entire people.

In the June election the Civic Forum confirmed its political ascendency by achieving almost 50% of the vote. The historical parties (the social democrats, socialists, etc.) were electorally wiped out, while the communist party came second with 13.6%. The newly created parties did badly, though surprises were achieved by Christian Democrats, Slovak separatists and Moravian autonomists, all of whom are represented in the new parliamentary bodies, sharing power (with the exception of the Slovak separatists) with the Civic forum.

Paris 1990

PART 2

7

CONSTITUTIONS AND PARLIAMENTS

The constitution passed in 1920 was in force in Czechoslovakia until May 9, 1948. This constitution was based on the legal system and procedures of the defunct Habsburg Monarchy and was then only slightly modified to suit new conditions in the Czechoslovak republic. The proclamation of independence by the National Committee of Prague, on October 28, 1918, was embodied in the constitution. On November 14, 1918, the National Assembly (Parliament) composed of Czech members of the Imperial Parliament and of co-opted members, passed a provisional constitution, which in 1919 was twice amended (Acts 138 and 271), but remained in force until 1920, when a new constitution was drafted and approved by the National Assembly.

On instruction from the President of Czechoslovakia, the Minister of the Interior formed a committee of experts and started work on the draft; the ministry team, of course, consulted freely with political parties and other bodies. On December 10, 1919, it passed its proposals to the special constitutional committee of the National Assembly. This committee discussed the draft for three months at fifteen sessions and prepared its own report to be submitted to the National Assembly alongside with the ministry draft: the Social Democratic members also submitted their minority reports. The Assembly then discussed the draft and the three reports, and finally accepted them all. On February 29, 1920, the constitution was voted by the Assembly and became law on March 6, 1920.

Thus, the constitution was a mixture of several constitutions, but as a basic law it certainly satisfied the needs of the new Czechoslovak state. Still in 1920 several of its chapters were re-drafted and improved by amendments passed by the Assembly in the form of constitutional laws, but otherwise it remained in force without substantial modification until the war in 1939. The constitution made Czechoslovakia a unitary state: the Czech and Slovak provinces were governed from Prague, while Ruthenia became autonomous. The President was the head of state as well as Commander-in-Chief of the armed forces; he had great administrative and executive powers. He was elected not by popular vote but by the two chambers, the senate and the chamber of deputies, of the Czechoslovak Parliament (National Assembly). Parliament was elected directly and secretly for a period of six years (the senate for eight). Political parties freely competed for the votes by submitting lists of candidates to the electorate. The President appointed a government which commanded a majority in the chamber of deputies, and dismissed it when it lost the confidence of the lower chamber. The system was finely balanced, each institution checking the other, and throughout the existence of the First Republic (1918–1939) it worked reasonably well. Basic freedoms were guaranteed in the constitution and existed in practice within the system. However, the Czechoslovak political system also had several weaknesses: too many parties competed for power and constitutional provisions for the protection of minorities seemed to work less satisfactorily. In the end, the latter problem brought about external intervention which resulted in the destruction of Czechoslovakia and its occupation by Hitler's Germany.

All constitutional liberties and rights were suspended in 1938 and the political system was all but destroyed by the Germans, during the war 1939–1945. The post-war system was radically different. Although the 1920 constitution was in force even after May 1945, the liberated country was essentially different. President Beneš, as constitutional head, made many important amendments to it. Thus in the form of presidential decrees, Dr. Beneš abolished the upper chamber, the senate, established purely elective local government, set up new courts, nationalized the greater part of industry, as well as disbanding all political parties which had collaborated with the enemy during the war. In fact Czechoslovakia went into an election in June 1946, so that the resulting parliament (Constitutional National Assembly) could draft and approve a new constitution.

A new political organization was created, the National Front, a sort of coalition of the parties allowed to participate in the new system, where policies were discussed and agreed to. At first all the renewed political institutions were worked by appointed people, but in 1946, after the election, the new system became representative. The political parties were proportionately represented, not only in parliament and government, but also in local government.

After the election in 1946 the National Assembly immediately set up a constitutional committee composed proportionately of all the parties represented in the Assembly, which then began to draft the new constitution. Although the drafting was held up on several occasions when the parties could not agree, the draft was almost completed when, in February 1948, the Communist Party seized power through a coup d'Etat. Curiously the Communist party did not substantially amend the draft, nor pass it through the intimidated (and to a certain extend truncated) National Assembly; instead it waited for a new election, resignation of the President and only then had it passed unanimously by the newly elected Assembly. Henceforth the legal basis of life in Czechoslovakia became the so-called May Constitution of 1948.

Evidently, during the drafting in the years 1945–48, constitutional experts and the constitutional committee of the Assembly had to face and resolve many difficult points. Thus, only a fraction of the 1920 constitution corresponded to reality: Paragraph 5 concerning Ruthenia was invalid, for this province had been ceded to the USSR. Paragraphs 6 and 7 concerning Slovakia were largely out of date: the Slovak National Council which established itself in Slovakia after the uprising in 1944 took over powers so far reserved for central government. Paragraphs concerning the senate, age qualifications of electors and candidates as well as the electoral court were inapplicable. With the abolition of the senate, the election of the President had to be modified; Paragraph 80 dealing with the central government had to be changed, too. Paragraph 86 concerning state administration became invalid, when national councils were set up, and Chapter 6 concerned with the protection of minorities became superflous, after almost all the minorities had been deported and expelled from the country. However, Chapter 5 containing rights and freedoms of the citizens was largely modified. The greatest problem the constitution had to resolve was the position of Slovakia in the republic, and the position of political parties which were involved in all the three classical components of the political system, the legislative, executive, and judiciary.

The resulting May Constitution was certainly a Communist one, but it was not of the "higher" Soviet type: it simply established another hybrid Czechoslovak system, the People's Democratic principle was the key to it: the people were the source of all power and power (legislative, executive, and judiciary) belonged to the people. The people governed themselves through elective representative organs (national committees [soviets], parliament and government). The basic constitutional principle of the people's democracy was further developed. The Communist Party, by assuming the leading role, in effect cancelled the democratic principles of representation and division of power.

The Communist Party wanted the constitution to reflect not only the status quo in Czechoslovakia, but also to serve as a source of future legislation, a "critical criterion" of the legal system as well as one of the power means for the democratization of the legal system; it no longer wanted the constitution to be the basic law of the state, from which all laws were derived. It was to be a political document, a people's charter as well as a declaration of political intention. A declamative part was added to the introduction, which was purely ideological and extolled the type of dictatorship of the Czechoslovak proletariat established by the Communist Party after the coup. Moreover, the basic articles which followed this introductory declamation shortly became theoretical, too; the third part of the constitution containing descriptive norms of the political system was also out of date by the end of 1948. While the Communist Party thought that it had achieved its revolution in February 1948 and proclaimed it solemnly in this constitution, it had actually just embarked on it. Thus, apart from its declamative parts, the 1948 constitution sorted out nothing and was out of date practically at the same time as it bacame law.

In 1968, when all the past was subject to criticism, Communist constitutional experts tore the constitution to pieces. The fusion of powers which the constitution allowed by upholding the principle of the Communist Party leadership in all affairs, was blamed for the excesses of the period of the cult of personality 1949–53. It was argued that, by allowing the offices of party leader and of President to fuse, it enabled President Gottwald to become Czechoslovakia's Stalin with all it meant. Gottwald transformed the government into the civil service, making all policy decisions himself and he took away from the National Assembly its powers of control. In this way he could exercize power and commit excesses without any restraint. In addition, the constitution also failed to sort out the nationality problem: it gave a measure of autonomy with its legislative assembly, the Slovak National Council, but no real executive, and since the Council was weakened as was its Czechoslovak counterpart in Prague, the National Assembly, Slovakia was in fact ruled as it had been previously, directly from Prague.

Although numerous objections were raised against this constitution, immediately after Gottwald's death in 1953 and especially after 1956, the successors of Gottwald, Zápotocký and Novotný, tried to cling to this "basic law" and above all to its practice, especially after 1957, when once again the office of party leader and President were fused. The restless Slovaks were purged, though not liquidated as was the case before. In the end, however, Novotný gave in to pressure, and in 1960 produced another constitution which was to tidy up Czechoslovak problems, and at the same time proclaim the Czechoslovak republic a socialist state a par with the USSR.

It was obvious that, by 1960, the 1948 constitution, even in its descriptive parts, did not correspond to Czechoslovak reality, so even constitutional experts saw a need for revisions. However, no one saw any urgent need for a new constitution. This was rather a political demand by President Novotný who reasoned that the new socialist constitution would enhance his international reputation and standing. Thus, in the end, the self-proclaimed fact that socialism was established in Czechoslovakia was the only innovation in the constitution. Since the Czechoslovak experts had to explain why they did not copy the Soviet constitution, they argued that socialism in Czechoslovakia developed in a special way and this accounted for the differences. The President remained the all powerful figure in Czechoslovakia, not titular head as in the other Communist states, and this ideological excuse pacified Novotný, especially since he could clearly see that the other Czechoslovak "differences" would not work in practice. The constitutional experts tried, for example, to restore some of the powers of the National Assembly as "this was a feature of the Czechoslovak revolutionary tradition;" the Slovak problem was, if anything, exacerbated, since Slovakia lost its remaining ministries and the Slovak National Council was further weakened by this change.

According to expert opinion, this constitution concentrated on a restatement of citizen rights and duties, as these had been most abused in the recent past, despite the 1948 constitution. The 1960 constitution no longer contained articles prohibiting the misuse of liberties, but did contain many categorical rights and duties. The difficulty was that these rights and duties were not formally defined, had often no legal basis nor institutional backing for their implementation. Society as such was expected to decide when these constitutional rights and duties were infringed and that was obviously impractical. Moreover, the legal position of the Communist Party was embedded in the constitution itself. It was no longer understood that the Communist Party as the strongest element of the National Front ruled the country. Similarly to the Soviet formula, the Communist Party became the leading force in society and in the state, being supreme in everything. Although Paragraph 6 mentioned the National Front as the political body of all workers from town and country led by the Communist Party, this was no longer the National Front coalition but an association of social and other organizations. A little paradoxically the Communist Party continued to share power with four other political parties, although these parties were not mentioned in the constitution and were not allowed to represent different interests and policies from those of the leading Communist Party. They simply represented social groups in politics—the Czech Socialist Party supposedly represented the Czech intelligentsia; the (Catholic) People's Party represented Catholic farmers (individual and collectivized) etc. In any case, this particular constitutional arrangement was contrary to that in the Soviet Union, where no organized political bodies were admitted into the ruling coalition of the Communist Party and the non-party citizens. Thus, it largely invalidated the declamative part of the constitution which proclaimed Czechoslovakia a socialist state a par with the USSR, or at least made this claim highly implausible.

However imperfect the constitution turned out to be, it would have satisfied another generation of Czechs and Slovaks, had it not been for the crisis through which the Czechoslovak Communist Party passed in 1968. As a result of this crisis, the leadership of the Communist Party was removed and replaced by another, which then vehemently attacked the 1960 constitution. In the action program of the Communist Party approved on April 5, 1968, the constitution was practically demolished and instructions were given to commence work on a new one. Thus, all the rights and duties of the Czechoslovak citizens were to be clearly defined and guaranteed by institutions, legal or otherwise. The National Front became again a coalition body, where political parties acted as partners and the leading role of the Communist Party was defined as moral leadership. Above all the new constitution was to resolve for ever and equitably the Slovak minority problem. However, before a draft could be made, the occupation of Czechoslovakia by the Warsaw Pact armies stopped work on it, and in the end nothing came of it.

Instead, the National Assembly passed a large number of constitutional amendments which form the basis of the present constitution. Act 100–1968 canceled Chapters 3–6 of the old constitution and transformed Czechoslovakia into a federal republic, consisting of two equal Czech and Slovak republics. Act 143–1968 defined and formalized this federation, while laws 144–1968 regulated the position of the nationalities within the federation. Act 10–1969 established the State Council of Defense and Act 126–1970 defined federal powers and administration, thus completing the transformation of Czechoslovakia. Despite the interruption caused in the drafting of the constitution by the occupation of the country, Czechoslovakia, alone in the Communist world remained constitutionally distinct: it did not have one constitution, but five constitutional laws forming its basis. In addition, many laws were passed by the Federal Assembly which have the force of constitutional amendments and are considered as parts of the constitution.

According to this composite constitution, Czechoslovakia is a social-ist state because it is based on the power of workers, farmers and intellectuals led by the Communist Party. It is also socialist because all its economy is nationalized, and it is a member of the Warsaw Pact and the Communist international system. The state is a republic headed by a President; both Czech and Slovak republics form the Federal Republic of Czechoslovakia. The President is elected by the Federal Assembly, which is a federal parliament consisting of two chambers: the People's Chamber elected directly, and the Nations Chamber consisting of equal numbers of Czech and Slovak deputies. Contrary to other Communist countries, the President is an individual and not a collective; the politi-cal system is multiple—political parties take part in it, although they all recognize the leading role of the Communist Party.

The basis of the state is formed by representative institutions elected by the people. The Federal Assembly is elected in parliamentary elec-tions which are direct, secret and whose candidates are selected by the National Front. Its special position in the system was abolished in 1970, after a law passed in 1968 was repealed. Each republic has also separate legislative bodies, the National Councils, which appoint and control republican executive governments, as does the Federal Assembly on the federal level. Local government bodies are also elected, but have admin-istrative services (civil service) to carry out their policies.

The President and the State Council of Defense are responsible for national security and defense; the former is Commander-in-Chief and declares war after consultation with the council and on approval by the Federal Assembly. Internal security is assured by the Corps of National Security (police) which is subordinated to the Ministry of the Interior and whose position is constitutionally undefined, being sufficiently explicit. Other bodies securing internal order are also left out of the constitution: the People's Militia, an "instrument of defense for the working class;" Fire Brigades and the Voluntary Guard of Public Order. The ultimate control over public order and observance or infringement of law belongs to the procuracy and courts, which are clearly defined in the various federal laws.

This new constitution transformed Czechoslovakia completely and was in many ways a break with the past. However, since 1968, while Czechoslovakia is formally completely different from what it was before, many past practices have been resumed after 1970. Thus, it will be pertinent to consider the legislature first, as it is the core of the Czecho-slovak political system, and point out its unique aspects, as well as putting it into correct perspective.

PARLIAMENTS

Since its inception in 1918 the National Assembly, or Parliament, has been the most important political institution in Czechoslovakia. In all the constitutions of Czechoslovakia (1920, 1948, and 1960) the National Assembly is described as the supreme representative body in which national sovereignty resides (Article 39, Paragraph 1). Apart from its unique legislative powers, it also has great controlling powers, and above all elects the head of state, the President, as well as the Supreme Court judges. By tradition, it is the vehicle to power: politicians of all parties enter parliament in order to achieve power, either in the executive (central government) or in the presidency. It is curious to note that the Communist politicians after their victorious coup in 1948, continued to respect and carry on with the tradition. Thus, before the coup, Communist deputies were also members of the party's central committee; the ministers whom the party chose from the deputies were automatically members of the party presidium. After the coup, in the 1948 election, there was a sudden influx of Communist leaders into parliament (especially those who had no chance to be elected in the conditions of pre-coup Czechoslovakia: A. Novotný, the future party leader and President, finally got elected. But other leaders also made their entry into "politics:" in December 1948, J. Hendrych entered the Assembly in a bye-election, followed by H. Leflerová, V. Knap, A. Dubček, etc. In subsequent parliaments every really ambitious Communist politician made sure that he was elected to the Assembly, even though after the years of the personality cult (1949–53) this body politic appeared fairly battered (some 150 members were purged): O. Homola reemerged, V. Škoda, B. Čakrtová, C. Hruška, J. Šejna, M. Vecker, O. Šimůnek, L. Štoll, R. Barák, V. Krutina, V. Kolář, V. Janko, P. Majlink, R. Cvik, S. Kodaj, J. Lorincz, V. Litvaj, K. Šavel, I. Rendek, and R. Strechaj got elected. In 1960, most of the reform leaders finally made the assembly: V. Koucký, V. Prchlík, B. Kučera (the liberal leader), L. Štrougal, K. Poláček, B. Lomský, A. Polednák, D. Kolder, O. Černík, J. Lenárt, E. Pepich, V. Bilák and others. Almost all the leaders of the 1968 reform movement became members of parliament in 1964, and their successors made sure that they were added to this body after the purges 1969–71 or in the 1971 election. President L. Svoboda had been a member of all parliaments since 1945.

Thus the unique and powerful position of the Assembly in the political life of Czechoslovakia was recognized even by the leaders of the Communist Party, who after all served their political apprenticeship in this body. This realization was expressed in a negative sense by the destructive effects of the personality cult, during the years 1948–53, on the National Assembly. In these long years the party was "afraid" of this institution, and purged it ruthlessly. Then it tried to muzzle it, and transform it into a perfect replica of the Supreme Soviet in the USSR. Though it overtly destroyed its competitive electoral basis in 1948, as well as procedural processes, and its committee system in 1950, it nevertheless failed to transform the Assembly into a Supreme Soviet: it remained a truncated Czechoslovak Parliament. Immediately after President Gottwald's death, the Communist Party decided to revive this important political institution, which still seemed to have a place within the new system. The problem was how to resurrect it? In 1953 President Zápotocký tried to infuse new life into it by personally attending its plenary sessions. In 1954, A. Novotný hoped that the election would revive the body. In December 1954, the central committee sought to achieve this by means of instructions to members of parliament, but they proved insufficient. In 1960, after some administrative reforms and a new constitution, the Communist Party made new decisions which were to "deepen socialist democracy" and increase the role of the National Assembly (central committee decisions of 13-14 January 1960 and 7-8 April 1960). However, these decisions failed to have the required effect. A public debate ensued as to the best way in which the Assembly should be revived: in 1962 the members of parliament themselves publicly discussed the new and improved methods of their work (RP February 16, 1962). Visible improvements only came after the 1964 election. In May of that year, the central committee finally decided on substantial changes in the working of the Assembly and on the restitution of its many controls. Henceforth it revived incredibly rapidly and came back full circle into its own during the short hectic months of 1968. Although after the occupation of Czechoslovakia, in August 1968, the National Assembly was purged and its political status slightly downgraded, the Federal Assembly of 1971 still retained greater powers and prestige than those Assemblies in the period 1948–68.

Structurally, the Communist Party changed the National Assembly only marginally between 1948–68; great structural changes did occur after the federal law had been passed (Act 143-1968). Thus the unicameral Assembly, established in 1945, remained unchanged after the coup in 1948 until 1949, when certain powers and importance of the plenary session were curtailed in favor of the Speaker and presidium, as in the USSR. Within this structure, only the presidium and the few remaining committees did really work, while the plenary session remained largely formal. In 1964 only did a major shift occur back to the pre-1949 arrangements: the presidium's powers were weakened, the committees still further strengthened and consequently the plenary session became lively and important again. Throughout 1968, this shift in emphasis was fully maintained, but soon structural changes brought about new and unprecedented conditions.

Throughout 1945–68, the Slovak province of Czechoslovakia had its own provincial parliament (Slovenská národná rada), but, because of fears of separatism, this body never really prospered and rapidly became an insignificant appendix of the National Assembly. In 1960 its existence reached its lowest depth when its executive branch (Poverenictvo) was abolished. However, in 1968 it was not only resurrected but also given new powers, so that it became a real legislative and controling body of Slovak autonomy, which it was supposed to be from the very beginning in 1944. In the federal reorganization of Czechoslovakia, the Slovaks also achieved another type of equality with the Czechs, by having a second chamber added to the Federal Assembly. The Nation's Chamber consists of an equal number of Czech and Slovak deputies and has a power of veto. In addition each republic (Czech and Slovak) has its own legislative body, which passes republican laws and controls its own republican executive.

It is curious to note that the new federal system, above all the legislative arrangements, though arising out of the reforms in 1968, departs almost completely from the historical arrangements and customs in Czechoslovakia, and closely resembles the Soviet system.

ELECTORAL LAWS

One factor that made the various Assemblies such a powerful institution was the law which governed their elections. The Czechs and Slovaks had a long, though differing, historical experience as far as electoral laws were concerned. Since 1907, (Act 15, February 26, 1907) the Czechs could elect their representatives to the central parliament (Reichsrat) on the basis of universal suffrage, directly and secretly. Only two minor qualifications prevented this Act from being fully democratic: every male over twenty-four could vote, provided he had been a resident in a constituency for over one year; the major one was that women had no voting rights. On the other hand, the Slovaks only got comparable voting rights after the collapse of Austria-Hungary in 1918.

Electoral arrangements were basically regulated in the Constitution of 1920, and in a series of Acts which modified certain procedures. In 1919 (Act 663) permanent electoral lists in all communes were made compulsory; twice every year, these lists were made public so that objections could be lodged or amendments made. Act 44 in 1920 only slightly completed Act 663. Acts 123 and 208 of 1920 regulated the election of the National Assembly. (Only slight changes to these two Acts were effected in 1925 and 1935.) The bi-cameral Assembly was elected on the basis of universal suffrage by all (male and female) citizens of Czechoslovakia over the age of twenty-one (over twenty-six for the Senate), who had resided in a constituency over three months. Thus vagrants, but also bankrupts and other convicted citizens were (or could be) disqualified from the vote. In 1927 (Act 56) members of the armed forces and gendarmerie were also disqualified. The other qualifications in 1920 were that candidates for the lower chamber had to be thirty years of age (for the Senate forty-five) and had to be citizens of Czechoslovakia for at least three years (for the Senate ten years).

Elections were organized by the Ministry of the Interior. The Ministry had to announce the election date at least twenty-eight days beforehand; electoral lists were displayed for fourteen days and candidates had to be nominated sixteen days before the election. The Ministry worked through electoral commissions: (1) local ones which compiled electoral lists; (2) district ones which organized the ballot and whose members were representatives of the parties or groups taking part in the election; (3) regional ones which supervized and amended electoral lists and checked results; and (4) a central commission appointed by the Minister (political parties had twelve members on it) which supervized the whole operation and announced final results.

There were no single constituencies but representation was proportionate. Every party or group received proportionate representation based on its vote. The defeated candidates in a given electoral district became substitutes in the order of poll. If a seat fell vacant, the next candidate on the list became automatically member. On the other hand members of parliament were not directly responsible to the electorate. The Constitution of 1920 (Paragraph 22) made members independent and they could not be recalled by their voters.

This perhaps complicated but rather fair system worked satisfactorily throughout the existence of the Republic of Czechoslovakia, 1918–39. A constitutional court which made the final decisions about elections was rarely in action and overall final results were never questioned. In 1925, some twenty-nine parties and groups competed in the general election, in 1929 nineteen, and in 1935 sixteen. Throughout this period, the Czechoslovak Agrarian Party emerged as the largest political party, with the exception of 1920 when the undivided Social Democrats won the election. The Communist Party consistently polled between 10-13 per cent of the total vote, but never joined the ruling coalition which consisted of the Agrarians, Social Democrats, Liberals, and Christian

Democrats. During the war 1939–45, no election took place. After the war, parliament was urgently required and was therefore elected on an extraordinary basis. President Beneš issued a decree (No 47) which had the force of a constitutional Act. It lowered age limits (eighteen for voters and twenty-one for candidates), abolished the senate and prescribed an emergency indirect election. Local electors were elected (one in 200—in Slovakia one per 500) who in turn elected land electors (Bohemia, Moravia, and Slovakia) and the land electors finally elected members of parliament and their substitutes. This Provisional National Assembly was elected in August 1945 and passed an electoral law (Act 67) on 11 April 1946, which regulated the election on May 26, 1946. This Act was largely based on the pre-war laws, and only aimed at slightly simplifying the system: the senate was definitely abolished and only four political parties were allowed to compete. The age regulations of the Presidential decree were incorporated in this Act. Under this system, the Communist Party became the largest single party and polled some 38 per cent of the total vote. No opposition party was permitted and the four competing parties ruled in a coalition called the National Front.

After the coup d'Etat in February 1948, new electoral arrangements were introduced in the Constitution passed in May 1948. Though four political parties still continued to 'compete', the system was considerably simplified. The National Front became responsible for the nomination of candidates, not the political parties as previously, and there was only one list of candidates for which to vote, that of the National Front in which the Communist Party obtained a disproportionate majority based on the successful coup. No opposition candidates were allowed to stand, but despite additional restrictions (no secret vote) some 20 per cent of voters voted against the National Front in 1948. This imperfect solution (from the Communist point of view) was not put to another test, while President Gottwald was alive. When the need for another election was felt, new laws were passed; they brought about the contemporary arrangements (Acts 26 and 27 in 1954, new provisions in the Constitution of 1960, Act 34 in 1964, Act 113 in 1967, and finally Act 43 in 1971).

For the first time in the history of Czechoslovakia, all elective assemblies and organs were elected for a period of five years. Though the 'socialist' Constitution of 1960 made provisions for a four year period, this has now been changed. The reason for this change seemed logical: since the Communist Party was acknowledged as the leading force in politics, it seemed appropriate that every election should follow party congresses which meet every five years. The party congress not only endorsed past policies, but also formulated future ones: thus, every future parliament will also have its policies prepared in advance. Every future election will be "fought" on a Communist Party program. Many of the traditional features of the electoral system were retained: every citizen of Czechoslovakia over eighteen (candidates twenty-one) must participate in an election, if he appears on electoral lists. Persons disqualified are the mentally ill or people in jail, or otherwise legally deprived. The differences from the pre-war system are in the process for the nomination of candidates. The 1948 innovation is in force: the National Front, which is an electoral bloc under the leadership of the Communist Party, combines other parties and social organizations and is responsible for nominations. Thus, even persons not belonging to any party can be nominated by the National Front as candidates and elected. The choice of candidates is made in electoral districts by district National Fronts, which then present the picked candidates to the electors and register them with the Czech and Slovak National Fronts. Candidates thus selected are elected by the voters. Electoral commissions at all levels are elected by the corresponding National Fronts, and not by representative bodies themselves as in the recent past. The Czech and Slovak National Fronts finalize the choice of candidates, when several nominations are made.

The election for the National (Federal) Assembly is by single constituencies and therefore candidates have to be selected beforehand, as no opposition is permitted. Though local elections take place simultaneously with the parliamentary election, more complicated rules apply: communes of up to 300 inhabitants elect councils of 9; 600: 11; 1,500: 17; 10,000: 40; 20,000: 60; 50,000: 85. District administration is also elected—80,000 inhabitants elect a 60-member council; above 80,000, 80-member councils: the regional councils elect at least 80-member councils. Constituencies for the bi-cameral Federal Assembly (Peoples and Nations Chambres) are announced by the presidium of the Federal Assembly at least sixty days before the election. The presidia of the Czech and Slovak National Councils similarly form their constituencies. For the Peoples Assembly, there are 200 constituencies and for the Nations Assembly 150 (75 in the Czech Republic and 75 and the Slovak Republic). For the Czech National Council, there are 200 constituencies, while for the Slovak one only 150. Constituencies contain approximately the same number of electors, with the exception of constituencies of the National Chambre, in which the Slovak representation is elected approximately by one-third of the Czechs. Electoral commissions, appointed by the corresponding National Fronts, organize the election at all levels; the central electoral commission of the National

Front is the highest and final authority.

Participation in the election is "morally" binding and everyone must cast his vote in person. An elector can either cast his vote directly, i.e. without any change; or he can cross out any candidate he does not approve of, in a room apart, specially provided for this purpose, in order to preserve the secrecy of choice. Candidates are elected if they poll more than one half of the votes. Elected members are responsible directly to their voters and can be recalled for various specified reasons by their electors. The corresponding National Front makes proposals in this respect, after testing public opinion at public meetings.

The Federal arrangements in Czechoslovakia required five new Acts to regulate the electoral system: Act 44 made provisions for the election of the Federal Assembly. Acts 53 and 54 regulated the elections in the Czech and Acts 55 and 56 in the Slovak Republics.

ELECTION 1948

After the coup d'Etat, the Communist Party of Czechoslovakia had no need to woo the electorate to sanction its political takeover in February 1948. Seemingly this approval and legitimization came from the Constitutional Assembly, where all political parties were represented, and approved the new government by 230 votes to 70 abstentions. Subsequently, the Congresses of Trades Unions and the Peasant Commissions gave them the social approval which they also needed. It speaks for the post-war system and historical tradition, that the Communist Party decided after a decisive victory to submit itself to the uncertain outcome of an election ordeal.

At first, the presidium of the Communist Party, which now made all political decisions, was inclined to make use of the existing electoral procedures as its leaders were convinced that they would win most decisively. Thus, in March 1948, it seemed that in the coming election the four Czech and four Slovak parties would put up separate lists of candidates, and that the Communist Party of Czechoslovakia would obtain between 65-70 per cent of the votes (on March 15, the estimate was 75 per cent overall). The difficulty these estimates presented to the Party presidium was that they varied widely from region to region, and in some provinces, Moravia and particularly Slovakia, could not be guaranteed at all. Thus, the Bohemian regions of Karlovy Vary and Ústí put their estimates as high as 90 per cent, Mladá Boleslav and Liberec 85 per cent, while the rest of Bohemia 75 per cent. After much hesitation and probably in view of the uncertainties in Moravia and Slovakia, the presidium decided that parties would not present their individual lists of candidates, but would all combine and put forward a United Front list. The decision was made public on April 5, 1948, and, four days later, it was endorsed by the party's central committee, which prior to the meeting had favored the election advocated by the regions.

Once the decision was made, it became a foregone conclusion that the Communist Party would score an overwhelming majority. The National Front which was no longer a coalition body but a cadre body which the party absolutely controlled, would nominate candidates and thus determine the composition of parliament. However, apart from this innovation, no great changes were planned and the Communist Party, together with other parties which were allowed to exist after the coup, participated in elections as a coalition. The immediate problem was to make sure that no significant numbers of voters cast their vote against the National Front candidates. On the very date of the election announcement, it became obvious that there would be electoral difficulties in the Ostrava and Olomouc regions; in these regions, as well as in Slovakia which the Communist Party hardly controlled at all, it seemed that a massive vote against the National Front would be registered. The Party, therefore, decided to make it as difficult as possible for its opponents. Election procedures were tightened up: instead of marking their ballot papers behind a screen, electors were "advised" to vote "publicly" and cast their votes in front of the election commissions, without availing themselves of the privacy of the screen. Tremendous organizational efforts went into the campaign, some 6,924 preelection meetings were held, at which new procedures were explained: thus the voters were being subtly or less subtly intimidated into voting for the National Front. The election took place on May 30, 1948, and the results proved most interesting. Some 6.5 per cent of voters failed to cast their votes, which was more than ever before, since Czechoslovak citizens were under legal obligation to vote. These abstentions were obviously a protest vote. The white votes amounted to some 770,000, which was 10.7 per cent of the electorate. As predicted, 228 communes voted against the National Front by more than 50 per cent. Of these 177 (84 per cent) had previously been controlled by the Catholic Peoples Party. The National Front scored nevertheless an overwhelming victory and polled some 89.3 per cent of the vote cast. On this united list of candidates, seven political parties presented themselves for election to parliament. But the party representation was fixed in the most arbitrary way by the presidium of the National Front, which compiled lists of candidates, on instructions from the Communist Party presidium. The Communist Party had 215 members of parliament (52 of them from Slovakia), when previously, in 1946, it had 114 members only. In this parliament 1948–54, it had a two-third majority (300 members were elected) and thus could constitutionally carry out any reform, or even abolish the system, if it wished so. The three Czech parties were ungenerously given a block of 23 members each. The Socialist Party's representation was thus halved (1946—55 members). The Catholic Peoples Party and the Slovak Democratic Party also suffered substantial losses (in 1946 they had 46 and 43 MPs), and even the Social Democrats came out of this election greatly reduced (1946—37 MPs). Only the Slovak Freedom Party increased its representation from 3 to 4 MPs.

The Assembly, which met for the first time on 10 June 1948, was, despite its artificial fixed representation, still a parliament, for the Communist Party was not yet sure how it would rule Czechoslovakia. Parliament still remained the only gate to power. All the government ministers stood as deputies for the election and were the first to swear allegiance to the Republic. Politically, it was still the most prestigious body; moreover, the Assembly was bent on continuing to organize its work in the traditional fashion. It elected its presidium and a perplexing number of committees and commissions, to enable itself to execize effectively its legislative and controlling powers.

The Communist Party had its most capable members elected, and party leaders were members of the government. The presidium elected on the first day was headed by a minority (Social Democratic) leader, Dr. O. John, and while it had a Communist majority, all the other parties, except the Slovak Freedom Party, had several members on it. This body was still only responsible for managing plenary sessions and preparing agendas. It retained a relatively large secretariat of civil servants, who not only secured the administration of the presidium business, but also of the Assembly and its committees and sub-committees. While committee and sessional minutes were supervized by members of parliament and approved by the Assembly, the secretariat kept detailed records of sessions, committee meetings and voting. Curiously, this secretariat survived almost intact all the ensuing changes that the National Assembly was subject to.

ELECTORAL CAMPAIGNS

Traditionally, elections in Czechoslovakia have been preceded by vigorous electoral campaigns. Though after 1948 the Communist Party curtailed the campaigns, nonetheless they were permitted and had a unique character. It is obvious, from the discussion of the electoral laws in force in Czechoslovakia, that quite a number of features of the pre-1948 system have been retained. The latest electoral campaign in November 1971, in spite of several new institutions, was on the whole typical. The election date was fixed two months in advance, so that an electoral campaign "could be prepared and conducted." The presidia of the Federal Assembly and the Czech and Slovak Councils made the election date known on September 27, 1971. Immediately, three types of electoral committees were set up: (1) electoral committees of the National Front at all levels (central, regional, district and local), whose task was to compile the lists of candidates; (2) electoral district committees organized by the Czech and Slovak National Councils; these committees organized electoral procedures and issued ballot papers; and (3) electoral district committees which supervized the ballot itself, provided buildings and rooms for the vote, counted the votes, and passed on the results to the central election commission. (There were 18,874 of these committees, with some 130,000 people involved, in the 1971 election.)

The election manifesto for 1971 was based on the resolutions and directives of the Fourteenth congress of the Communist Party of Czechoslovakia, which took place in May 1971. All the branches of the National Front took this manifesto as the basis for their electoral statements. The manifesto was presented to the electorate together with the candidates. Electoral meetings took place during the first month of the campaign. There are no national figures of these meetings but the North Moravian Region published its own: between September 5 and 30, 1971 the regional Communist Party organized meetings attended by 302,650 citizens; some 30,000 questions were asked by the participants. At these meetings people could not only object to the election manifesto (no one actually did!) but also to the candidates. No modifications to the manifesto were suggested and all the candidates were approved: consequently, they were officially registered by the district committees and their names printed on the ballot papers.

In the next phase, agitation centers were set up all over Czechoslovakia: some 7,867 in 1971, as contrasted with some 5,000 in 1964. These printed election manifestoes and other literature were distributed among the population. They also organized agitator duets (dvojice), election agents going in twos, whose task was to visit every household in the country and ask for its support. This task was fulfilled on October 22-24, 1971, when practically every citizen was visited by these "duets." The rest of the campaign consisted of election meetings, addressed by registered National Front candidates who attempted to convince electors that they were the right persons to represent them, and carry out election promises contained in the manifesto.

For the ballot itself, each elector was issued with an election card. On arriving at the election room, he was checked against the electoral list and then given the ballot paper. The paper (or rather papers, for each elector voted simultaneously in the local, regional, and national election) contained the name of the registered candidate: voters voted for the candidate by placing the ballot paper in the ballot box. To vote against the candidate, the elector had to cross off the name of the candidate. This presumably required him to retire behind a screen where he could effect the modification. But this seemed dangerous. Electoral commissions could duly take note of such an elector, for all the citizens were asked by the National Front to vote publicly for its candidates: 99.81 per cent preferred to vote this way.

Even from this incomplete analysis of the campaign, it is obvious that every election in Czechoslovakia is a great organizationsl feat. In 1971, for the first time, all candidates were elected to all the appropriate council, parliamentary or local government bodies. The Communist Party proved that it could undertake any political task and ensure the greatest possible success. In this way, it could consult the people without necessarily giving them the widest possible choice.

COMMITTEE SYSTEM

The system of parliamentary committees and commissions (these are ad hoc bodies while the former are permanent) is the traditional way in which the Czechoslovak National Assembly has always set about its business. Even after the simplifications following World War II, the Constitutional Assembly (1946–48) abounded in committees and sub-committees. The most important committee in this parliament was the constitutional one (Act 197—October 17, 1946) which consisted of thirty-six members and was to achieve the principal task of this Assembly, drafting a new constitution. Between 1946 and 1948, this committee held twenty meetings and finally presented the draft of the constitution to the newly-elected Assembly in May 1948.

Apart from this chief committee, some twenty-two other committees and commissions functioned in the period of the Constitutional Assembly. The Verification Committee (held five meetings) confirmed the validity of members' election; the Permanent Committee (one meeting) looked after the business of parliament as such; the Incompatibility Committee (one meeting) looked into the business interest of members, and made sure that they were not contrary to the constitutinal laws. However, these were on the whole quiet bodies; other committees were kept fairly busy. Thus the Foreign Affairs Committee (twenty-four members) held twenty-three meetings, the Agricultural Committee (thirty members) seventy-four meetings, while the Trade and Commerce Committee held thirty-nine meetings. The Immunity Committee (eighteen members), which was entitled to lift parliamentary immunity from members, met nineteen times, while the Cultural Committee (twenty-four members) met twenty-five times. The Army Committee (twenty-four members) was kept rather busy at twenty-nine meetings, while the Security Committee was even busier with thirty-one meetings, during which matters of national security were discussed and decided upon. It can be said that every member of parliament sat on at least one committee; committees met in intervals between plenary sessions, and the latter were quite frequent. A member of parliament was kept fully occupied and members certainly earned their parliamentary salaries.

It seems obvious that, even after the coup d'Etat in February 1948, and the restricted election in May 1948, the Communist Party could think of no better way than to continue parliamentary activity, on practically the same basis as before. At the first plenary session of the new Assembly, committees were elected. Though their number was slightly reduced, they still covered all the important aspects of national life, and it was obvious that they would not only discuss and formulate policies, but also prepare legislation and exercize control in their respective fields. The separate committees, Army and Security, were united and kept under the control of the secretary general of the Communist Party, R. Slánský, who became chairman. Another important committee, Agriculture, was chaired by another influential Communist leader J. Smrkovský. The Foreign Affairs Committee came under V. Nový, Legal and Constitutional under Dr. Bartuška, Cultural under Koubek, Budget under Válo, Economic under Mrs. Mouralová, and Trade and Commerce under Horn. The Communist Party, as the strongest in this parliament, took over decisive control of all the vital committees: only several unimportant ones (the corresponding ministries were controlled by the same party) were left to members of other parties. Thus the Social Democrats chaired the Food Committee (Mrs. Jungwirthova) and Control and Savings Committee (Lindauer) while the Socialists chaired the Social Security and Health Committee (Matl). Christian Democrats chaired the Incompatibility Committee (Dr. Batěk) and Control of the Two year Plan Committee (Dr. Berák). The Slovak Democrats, now renamed as the Slovak Revival Party, chaired only one committee, the Initiative Committee (Dr. Štefánik), which clearly indicated that very little initiative would be left to this committee.

It appears that in the initial period of this parliament, most of these committees were kept very busy, because between June 1948 and October 1949 the Assembly passed a record number of laws, which transformed Czechoslovakia into a Communist state and the Assembly itself into a body resembling the Supreme Soviet. Unfortunately, no analysis of committee meetings is available; by then, committee proceedings had become state secrets and were no longer published. In this parliament, there was an additional reason for frequent committee meetings. According to the new constitution, members of the Assembly were no longer full-time paid members; they retained their previous jobs and were only paid for the missed working hours of their employment. However, the Speaker and the presidium members were still full-timers and were paid full parliamentary salaries. Members of committees were paid special allowances for attending committee meetings, and since the important committees met very frequently, they were still full-time paid parliamentarians.

It is not clear when wholesale simplifications of the committee system did occur. In June 1948, some sixteen committees were formed and members elected to them. In October 1949, when new procedural rules were introduced into the Assembly, the system of committees was probably also modified. Six committees disappeared altogether and the remaining ten were substantially reorganized to cover additional fields. The Army and Security Committee continued to exist (thirty members) under R. Slánský's chairmanship, but it disappeared soon afterwards, together with its chairman, who was tried and executed for high treason. The Foreign Affairs Committee only changed its chairman: Dr. V. Procházka was substituted for V. Nový, who had been arrested and remained in prison for some time. Other committees retained their initial chairmen: the Economic Committee (Mrs. Mouralová), the Cultural Committee (L. Koubek), the Agricultural Committee (J. Smrkovský), soon to be arrested and imprisoned, the Budget Committee (J. Válo), the Social Security and Health Committee (J. Mátl), the Constitutional and Legal Committee (Dr. J. Bartuška). The Immunity Committee was transformed into the Mandate Committee and Dr. L. Kokeš remained its chairman, though he probably had precious little to do with the immunity of members; the most vigorous purge of the Assembly was launched at this stage. The Control of the Two Year Plan Committee was transformed into the Committee of Economic Planning and Control, and remained under its Christian Democratic chairman, Professor Dr. J. Berák. These changes indicated that parliamentary committees lost almost entirely their former powers of control; they also ceased to discuss policies and bills. Draft bills must be presented directly to the Assembly, at its plenary meetings, which took place at monthly intervals. Bills were passed almost without any discussion.

After the election in 1954, which took place at the end of the personality cult period, everyone hoped, above all the members, for a revival of parliament and hence of its committees. But these expectations were not fulfilled. Although the new Speaker became Z. Fierlinger, an old parliamentarian (member of the Communist Party presidium), and even the first secretary and presidium member, A. Novotný, was elected to the parliamentary presidium, instead of revival, the process of simplification was continued; above all, the work of the Assembly and the committees themselves was still further paralyzed by the influx of new, inexperienced members. In 1954, only seven committees were formed and their membership was restricted (in 1957 practically all of them doubled their memberships). The Mandate Committee with eleven members was chaired by J. Vodička, originally a professional butcher. The Cultural Committee, now intended to supervize "cultural industries," had nineteen members and was presided over by Jan Drda, the "official" writer. The Economic and Budget Committee with twenty-seven members was chaired by J. Štětka, a glass worker, while the Agricultural Committee was run be V. Krutina, professional party organizer, soon to become Minister of Agriculture. Only the committees chaired by non-party members were composed of suitably qualified deputies, but, as a consequence, were of little political significance. Professor Dr. J. Berák (Christian Democrat) chaired the Foreign Affairs Committee, while Professor Dr. K. Káčl (Liberal/Socialist) chaired the Health Committee. Another expert lawyer, Dr. J. Krofta, chaired the Constitutional and Legal Committee which, however, had very little to do.

Only in 1957 did the Communist Party begin to think of really reviving the Assembly. To start with, parliamentary committees doubled their membership, so that a reasonable proportion of members would take part in parliamentary work. In 1960, the party's wish for revival and better use of the committees became public knowledge, but, on the whole, this had little effect on the National Assembly after the election in 1960. Only one new committee (for industry) was formed and other committees were strengthened by having as their chairmen important party leaders. J. Harus chaired the Mandate Committee, I. Skála the Cultural Committee, J. Válo the Plan and Budget Committee, J. Borůvka the Agricultural Committee, V. Škoda the Constitutional and Legal Committee, H. Leflerová the Foreign Affairs Committee, while the new Committee for Industry was chaired by an expert, A. Bichler. The Health Committee only was controlled by the non-Communist

Slovak, A. Žiak, while the rest was presided over by Communist leaders who were at least members of the party's Central Committee. It was during this period, 1960–64, that the Communist Party allowed public debates on the role of parliament and finally decided on strengthening its powers and prestige. The party also invited non-Communists to present their own proposals and a comprehensive package was subsequently approved at the Twelfth congress of the Communist Party in 1962. The effects of this "package" were to be felt after the election in 1964.

At the first plenary session after the election, on 12 June 1964, the new Assembly formed eleven committees: the Mandate Committee (twelve members) was chaired by the Christian Democratic member, M. Pospíšil, while the Committee for Trade, Services, Communications and Consumer Industries (twenty-eight members) was chaired by a Liberal, L. Dohnal. The Health Committee (twenty-six members) was presided over by a non-party professional, Dr. A. Petrusová. The rest of them were chaired by important party members, some of whom were going to play an important part in the liberalization of the system in 1968. Dr. V. Škoda, former Minister of Justice, and a rigid central committee member, controlled the Committee for Legal and Constitutional matters, while another, Mrs. Leflerová, presided over the Committee for Local Councils. The Foreign Affairs Committee was under the control of the "liberal" central committee member, Dr. F. Kriegel, while another "liberal" communist, A. Poledňák, chaired the Committee for Culture. An experienced deputy, F. Tymeš, chaired the Committee for Plan and Budget, while A. Bichler retained the chairmanship of the Committee for Industry and Transport. The Slovak Communist G. Gabruška, controlled the Committee for Investments and Building, and V. Kučera chaired the Committee for Agriculture and Food. Often the vice-chairmen of the committees, headed by Communist members, were non-Communists, and non-Communist representation on the committees was striking. The membership of the committees was increased; they averaged twenty-five members, thus giving every member of this parliament a chance to perform parliamentary duties on at least one of them. Committees encompassed almost the whole of national life, except the army and security, which still remained under the exclusive control of the Communist party's central committee, the so-called Eighth Department.

In April 1968, changes began to be felt even in this "liberal" National Assembly. Though the Novotnyite deputies refused to resign, the Speaker, B. Laštovička, and the presidium did stand down. J. Smrkovský, the reformer, was elected Speaker and the newly elected presidium also wanted reforms and changes; the frequency of their meetings more than doubled and in June and December 1968 they met every day, almost without interruption. Only one new committee was created, for Army and Security, and was chaired by an experienced Communist, L. Hofman. Another Committee, Peoples Control, was taken away from the government's jurisdiction and became a parliamentary committee. But otherwise no great changes were made in the structure and procedures of the committees, though judging from the large number of committees in the newly established Czech and Slovak National Councils, new committees were also envisaged for the National Assembly which became the Federal Assembly on January 1, 1969.

The election for the new federal system did not take place in 1968, and was delayed until November 1971, when the Communist Party considered the country sufficiently "normalized." After the election, when the newly elected Federal Assembly and the councils formed their committees, it became clear that the new régime would continue the 1964–68 practice of allowing all the legislative assemblies to work through their committees. In the Federal Assembly, each chamber formed eight committees, which included the Army and Security one. Completely new people were elected to preside over the committees, and only two of them were members of the party's central committee: Dr. Pennigerová, in the Social Security Committee (Peoples Chamber) and Dr. Auersperg, the Foreign Affairs Committee (Nations Chamber). Dr. Nejezchleb, a complete newcomer (formerly chairman of the Sports Association) was elected chairman of the Army and Security Committee and his counterpart in the Nation's Chamber became Dr. Mandʼák, member of the party's Central Control Commission. Both National Councils elected nine committees each. In the Czech Council, two committees were put under non-Communist chairmen (Committee for Trade and Transport: F. Toman, Christian Democrat; Health and Social Security Committee: V. Jedlička, Liberal-Socialist). The rest were chaired by party leaders, none of whom, however, reached central committee status. The Slovak National Council elected nine chairmen, all of whom were Communist Party members; non-Communist leaders (J. Gajdošík and Dr. M. Žákovič) were elected as Deputy Speakers of the Council.

LAWS AND LEGISLATIVE PROCESSES

Legislative processes in Czechoslovakia are rooted in ancient historical traditions and are in many ways unique. Because of the party system, individual deputies have always been less important than parliamentary party clubs. Thus questions (interpellations) in the Assembly have never been asked by individuals, nor did individuals advance bills (private member's bills do not exist): it has always been a party group which either asked questions or initiated legislation.

Legislative initiative often did not even originate from the parliamentary party, but from the political party as such. To demonstrate this unique Czechoslovak way of legislating, let us consider the following example: in 1934 the Social Democratic Party wanted a new social insurance act, covering all the working population in Czechoslovakia. Ideas for such a law were first voiced at a party conference and then discussed by the party presidium. The party presidium then engaged in talks with other parties, especially members of the ruling coalition. Afterwards, the party put its propsals to the Minister of National Insurance, who was also a member of the Social Democratic Party. The minister asked civil servants to prepare a bill, which he subsequently presented to parliament. The relevant parliamentary committee discussed the bill, amended it and returned it to the ministry for amendment. After it had passed through this stage, the Speaker presented the bill to a plenary session which then passed it and it became a law after it had been signed by the President and published in the statute book of Acts (Sbírka zákonů). It is a long and sometimes cumbersome way of passing laws, but it seems to have worked well between 1918 and 1939, and again from 1945 to 1948, so as to satisfy the citizens of Czechoslovakia. After the Communist coup in 1948, the Communist Party hardly altered the process: the initiative stage was slightly simplified, but otherwise all remained unchanged. The party, or its central committee, discusses ideas for a new law; the party presidium then instructs the relevant ministry to prepare a bill, which is presented to the parliamentary committee to be discussed, amended and possibly returned to the ministry for redrafting. When finally the bill is passed by the Assembly plenary session (with or without division—unanimously), it is promulgated in the customary constitutional way. In addition to this simplification (the party takes the initiative throughout), the Communist Party introduced two other modifications: in 1962 it established party commissions which generated ideas for new legislation; and the relevant departments of the Communist Party prepared these ideas in the form of proposals for the presidium and the ministry.

It should be stressed that since the establishment of the Communist regime, in February 1948, the Assembly was kept extremely busy with discussing and passing laws. While it is impossible to gauge the activity of the Assembly and its committes (committee proceedings are state secrets and are not published, a pre-war regulation), it is clear from the number of laws passed that the Communist Party wanted to use the

Assembly to accomplish all its political projects. Perhaps a little paradoxically, the busiest parliament proved to be the one elected in 1948. This Assembly counted among its achievements the dissolution of the pre-1948 system, its own dissolution into a Supreme Soviet, as well as passing the greatest number of laws ever, over 332 Acts. Some of these laws were unimportant (Act 32 dealt with the establishment and finance of theaters; Act 43 agricultural credits, etc.), but most of them were of a fundamental nature. Thus Act 46 dealt with agricultural reforms which had far-reaching effects, while Act 114 meant further nationalization and had a tremendous impact on the further development of industry. Act 118 nationalized wholesale trade and Act 120 all businesses with more than fifty employees. Acts 181, 183, 187, and 199 reorganized the money market, investment banks, cooperatives and communal enterprises. Act 280 reorganized the country's administration, replacing the historical land division with regions, while Act 286 reorganized the police and security. The security of the new system was embodied in Act 231, which introduced quite a number of new crimes against the state and increased penalties for them. Act 247 established labor camps, in which those convicted under the previous Act could serve their sentences. Act 319 reorganized the judiciary: in the terms of this Act, any citizen could be appointed judge by the Ministry of Justice. Act 322 reorganized barristers and solicitors, destroyed their independence and made them employees of a state organization. Many Acts regulated the economy, foreign trade and even artists' titles and it is obvious that at least the parliamentary committees must have sat almost continuously.

It is true that in 1949 this feverish activity abated a little, but all the same some 280 Acts were passed by the Assembly, several of them of the most fundamental nature. Act 60 was the most important one: it dealt with economic planning in Czechoslovakia. Several Acts (76, 87, 139) dealt with the administration of the capital, of local and district units, while Act 260 reorganized national insurance. In addition, agricultural collectives were given a legal basis, and research and documentation centrally organized (Act 261). In 1949 the Assembly also passed revised procedures and these for a long time put an end to "executive" legislation (they were revised again in 1954). The new procedures not only simplified the passing of Acts by the Assembly—its presidium was given increased legislative powers—but also limited plenary sessions and debates.

It is not surprising that in 1950 "only" some 191 Acts were passed and none of these was really important. Act 31 changed the status of the Czechoslovakia State Bank, Act 150 similarly treated the Czechoslovak Post Office. Doctors were newly organized (Act 197), insurance reorganized (Act 190) and peace was taken out of controversy, elevated to a law: any war propaganda made punishable by law (Act 165). In 1951, when only some 128 Acts had been passed, the legislators concentrated on tying up loose ends in legislation passed during the two previous years. The nationalized building industry was reorganized (Act 58) as well as nationalized shops and trading enterprises (Act 64). Act 68 regulated the status of voluntary organizations and gatherings. The Ministry of State Control was established (Act 73), as well as other ministries and Slovak ministries (proverenictva) (Acts 74, 75). Universities were reorganized (Act 80), state farms were established (Act 82) as well as tractor stations (Act 82). New laws were passed governing the professions of barristers, solicitors and notaries (Acts 114, 115, 116). Act 69 reorganized the protection of state borders, which until then had not required any special legislation. In 1952 the legislators concentrated on such important activities as fishing (Act 62), sea shipping (Act 61), on the establishment of the Academy of Sciences (Act 52) and Academy of Agricultural Sciences (Act 90), and this seems to have exhausted them for that year.

However, three Acts passed in the year 1952 were of fundamental importance: Act 64 once again reorganized and put on a new basis the courts and the procuracy, while Acts 65 and 66 dealt specificallly with the structure of courts and the procuracy. Although the number of Acts passed by the Assembly in 1953 (some 115) surpassed that of 1952, they were all without exception quite unimportant. Act 31 dealt with primary education and teachers training, Act 79 was really a supplement to a law governing the title of national artists, Act 81 put local government (Communist self governing councils) under the direction of central government, while Act 115 regulated authors' rights. In 1954, the Assembly passed several laws modifying electoral laws governing elections to the Assembly, the Slovak National Council as well as local councils (Acts 12, 13, 26, 27) and quickly passed into history, leaving behind a jungle of "laws" and an utterly "exhausted" (purged) Assembly.

In 1954 the new Assembly started auspiciously with a new set of procedural rules. It was hoped that, by re-emphasizing committee work, the Assembly would revive and possibly become the political instrument it once was in 1948 (Acts 61, 62). These re-establishment efforts, however, seem to have exhausted the legislative body, and all the repressive "laws" of the period of personality cult remained in force, unamended. The 1954 Assembly soon proved that even when committees were revived the Assembly as a body was not. Plenary sessions were rarely convoked, and the presidium still held the control and balance in its own hands. The Assembly passed some fifty-one Acts in 1955; none of which proved very significant. They ranged from the usual Plan for 1955 (Act 12) to the establishment and dissolution of research institutes (Act 14), the statute of spas (Act 43), and of nationalized enterprises (Act 51). However, in the same year, the presidium itself passed some sixty-four "legal measures" which all had the force of law: legal measure 21 established the presidium of the Supreme Court; 22 established wood inspection; 23 dealt with poisons; 58 covered children's allowances; 59 regulated salary rate for judges, procurators and probationary lawyers; 61 amended the divorce law; 64 amended the Health Act 103 (1951) and medical care therein. Even though in 1956 the Assembly passed more laws (some sixty-nine) than the presidium "legal measures" (some sixty-one), the presidium still dominated legislative activity and it became obvious that this Assembly would not recover from the blows dealt to it by the personality cult. However, the Acts passed in 1956 indicate the start of a process of recovery. Act 33 once again tackled Slovak administration and strengthened its autonomy. Act 40 dealt with the protection of nature, 45 shortened the labor week, 46 amended the law on universities, 47 dealt with civil aviation, while in Act 55 social security was tackled again. However, more important Acts came later in that year, possibly as a result of the Twentieth Communist Party congress in the USSR. Act 63 revised the criminal justice law of 1950; Act 64 amended criminal procedures, Act 65 reorganized courts; and Act 69 revised the tax system. These were all important and fundamental Acts, while the presidium "legal measures" dealt with limited but concrete problems (e.g. Numbers 30 and 31 regulated teachers' and doctors' salaries respectively).

In 1957 "reform" Acts continued to be passed (some eighty-two). Act 10 amended the Act dealing with national committees (local government and local administration); Act 14 amended the criminal administrative law (88-1950), while Act 24 covered thieving and pilfering of nationalized property. Act 26 fixed notaries' charges, Act 32 covered national health care for armed forces, and Act 35 dealt with technical co-ordination. Act 34 regulated the election of peoples and professional judges, while Act 37 defined their powers and responsibilities. Act 53 amended the statute of the Academy of Science, while Act 70 established the Institute of Social Sciences attached to the central committee of the Communist Party. Act 75 regulated identity cards and Act 76 amended the residential regulations of Czechoslovak citizens and foreigners.

In 1958, the Assembly passed some eighty-nine Acts while "legal measures" amounted only to some thirty-two. Act 16 amended the statute of the Czechoslovak Red Cross, Act 41 social security, Act 43 the

State Bank and Act 64 currency regulations. Act 40 regulated the income of imprisoned citizens and Act 67 regulated the inter-relations of Communist countries. Two important economic Acts were passed in this year, both regulating planning in nationalized industries and territorial planning. Last but not least, Act 87 systematized housing and building regulations. The year 1958, however, is interesting from another point of view. While previously the information media gave publicity to only the most important plenary sessions of the Assembly, henceforth they pay systematic attention to this body and its activity. Between 1948–54, the National Assembly held some thirty-eight plenary meetings; hardly any had been reported in the communication media. Between 1954–60, some thirty-eight plenary meetings took place and since 1958 they commanded the attention of the press at least. Of the eight plenary meetings taking place in 1958, five were reported in the press (Rudé právo of January 24, July 4, October 17 and December 13, 1958). During 1959, this attention increased still further: of the eight plenary meetings of that year, six were extensively covered in addition to one presidium meeting (the presidium held six meetings) and one committee meeting (foreign affairs). In 1960 there were only three plenary meetings and all three were reported in the press together with a presidium appeal to the Supreme Soviet of the USSR on the international situation and disarmament.

Between 1960–64, the Assembly passed through a phase of substantial recovery, though it "recovered" fully only after 1964. The presidium still animated and held some fifty-seven meetings while plenary sessions amounted to twenty-six, which was an average of six sessions a year. Throughout this Assembly plenary sessions were reported, sometimes in great detail. In April 1961 Rudé právo reported not only the jubilant debates of the successes of the FYP, but also the newly-passed law on the defense of Czechoslovakia and on the establishment of peoples courts (RP April 18 and 19, 1961). In June 1961, detailed accounts of the session reported the adoption of new laws: they dealt with the Central Office of State Control and Statistics, national committees (further amendments), public order, protection of health and the new organization of courts (RP June 27 and 28, 1961). In September 1961, the Prosecutor General's report to the Assembly on socialist legality was given publicity (September 20, 1961), while a month later the new penal code was publicized as well as routine economy debates dealt with (RP November 20, 1961). By contrast, the year 1962 meant a relative decrease of interest in the Assembly. Only two plenary meetings and debates were reported extensively (RP February 22 and March 30, 1962), but two committee meetings were given publicity. In 1963, all the meetings were given detailed publicity (RP January 25, March 7, July 10, September 26, December 5 and 6, 1963) as well as the three last plenary meetings in 1964 (RP January 31, February 27 and June 5, 1964). Throughout this session, the presidium still dominated the Assembly and plenary sessions tended to pass laws in batches (for example, six laws were passed on July 10, 1963). This state of affairs continued even after the Communist Party's congress late in 1962, at which decisions were made to increase the powers and political role of the National Assembly. The real implementation of this decision took place after the general election on June 2, 1964.

On June 24 and 25, 1964, the first plenary session of the Assembly elected a new presidium, approved the government program and elected an increased number of committees. When in September 1964 the second session took place, Mrs. Leflerová announced new powers and improved conditions for the work of the National Assembly to the deputies as well as the country (RP September 25, 1964). Ministers who attended this session also promised improved performance. Krajčír promised a better plan, Dvořák better finance, and Neuman better justice. In October 1964, the foreign affairs committee's meeting was publicized and the two-day debate of the plan and budget in December 1964 received detailed coverage (RP December 10 and 12, 1964). Though the Assembly was launched with a bang, there was no noticeable difference in its activity in 1965. Four plenary sessions took place in that year which passed several important laws: the Sixth plenary meeting passed a new labor code, social security legislation, while the Eighth session reorganized central administration, economy and improved the position of the Slovak National Council. More significantly, the Assembly refused to pass three bills: the one dealing with authors' fees, the others with vehicle tax and the amended criminal code. The bills went back to committees and thence to the government department for redrafting. This was indeed something quite unprecedented and indicated that, at long last, the Assembly was taking itself seriously. It was a return to the ways and atmosphere immediately after the coup d'Etat, and even prior to it.

In 1966 the Assembly again held the prerequisite number of plenary sessions (four), but the debates were lively and once again proved unprecedented. The university bill, health bill and other bills were debated in the keenest fashion, which made it quite clear that the presidium had lost its firm control on the debates, agenda and choice of speakers. Debates in committees and plenary sessions resulted in amendments and even redrafting. Moreover, questions were asked by individual deputies, thus reviving the old custom of interpellations:

members asked numerous questions about the development of the capital, Prague, and shortcomings in the national economy. While the ministers concerned were under constitutional obligation to produce answers to these questions, they successfully evaded the responsibility. In 1967 the Assembly held four plenary meetings, at which debates continued to be lively, while in the committees, hard struggle with the government continued. The agriculture committee returned to the Ministry of Finance its bill on agricultural tax and collectives' contributions to the national health service. The Legal and Constitutional committees criticized a bill on the rights of assembly, for which prior application was necessary. The Police Act was passed by 115 to 87 votes only after an amendment on parliamentary immunity was added. But, as J. Smrkovsky, Speaker in 1968, put it, many laws were passed against the better judgement of the Assembly, in the name of party discipline.

Although in the short months of 1968 the National Assembly finally resumed all its historical powers, all the same the "liberal" period 1964–68 bears a very favorable comparison with them. The secretary general of the Assembly office, Dr. V. Kaigl, summerized most aptly this period:

"As a result of the Communist Party's decisions in 1964, the deformations in the relations between the party and parliament have been put right. Immediately the central committee ceased to issue detailed instructions to parliament, the neglected three hundred (deputies) began to perform their tasks in earnest. On the positive side, the Assembly was responsible for the restructuring of industry, agriculture, house building and protection of environment. On the negative side, it still accepted too many easy explanations from the executive, which tolerated no control in defense and security fields."

However, in 1968 these negative points were put right and many more with them. Needless to say that, after 1969, after Husák's assumptions of power, all the improvements were quietly dropped and after 1971 the representative assemblies went back to the shape and functions of Novotný's early days. The Federal legislature existed formally until its reform in 1990.

8

CENTRAL GOVERNMENT
UNDER COMMUNISM

Since its inception in 1918, Czechoslovakia has been governed by coalition government. One consequence of this arrangement was that cabinet government or inner cabinet was not developed, although it was tried for a short time. The other consequence is that the government has never become too powerful; it always contained uneasy partners who put effective brakes to power ambitions. It was, rather, a platform for compromises and control over individual departments. The government met as a body as was required (once a week or month), made collective policy decisions and controlled their execution.

Individual ministers, however, have always exercised great powers. Once the government had made a compromise policy decision, it was the minister's task to implement it. He not only supervized the administration of policies through the civil servants, but also tried to avoid control of his actions by his colleagues in Parliament, or the President. Controls not only limited his power, but also led to questions, censures and political difficulties which usually resulted in restriction and a crisis. Not many crises occurred between 1918 and 1948, and the last one occurred on February 20, 1948, when members of the government resigned in protest against police measures taken by the Minister of the Interior, V. Nosek, and sparked off the coup d'Etat by the Communist Party of Czechoslovakia. Naturally, the political composition of the government has always been of primary importance. Before the coup d'Etat non-Communist political parties controlled the majority of departments of state, of which the government was composed. In the first two governments after World War II, the Prime Minister was a Social Democratic Party leader, Z. Fierlinger, and non-Communists (including the two non-party experts, Jan Masaryk and General Ludvík Svoboda, ministers of Foreign Affairs and Defense, respectively) controlled 15 out of the 22 ministries. After the election of 1946, the Communist leader, Klement Gottwald, became Prime Minister, but the Communist Party continued to control only seven ministries out of 24. The coalition government continued its existence even after the coup d'Etat, though the victory of the Communist Party was reflected in the composition of the government: it now controlled 13 ministries out of 22. Other political parties were given only token representation by the National Front: Social Democrats controlled four ministries; Czech Socialists two; Czech People's Party two; Slovak Revival Party one. Henceforth, over the years, even this token representation and sharing of power declined and reached a low in 1971, when the non-Communist parties failed to obtain any representation in the Federal government formed after the general election.

After the coup in 1948, the political control of ministries became much less important. The Communist Party now had an absolute majority in the government and, in any case, the ministers were chosen for their loyalty to the Communist Party, even the non-Communist members of government. Moreover, the civil service as a professional body was abolished and ministries became curious political-administrative bodies, executing policies decided upon at central committee meetings or Party presidium sessions. It was no longer important who was the minister (Communist or non-Communist), for he made no decisions but only supervized the execution of policies by his staff. The officials responsible for the execution of policies were handpicked Communists, usually factory workers, who were thought to be the most loyal Party members. They formed a local branch in the ministry and subjected it, and the minister, to the tightest political control. In practice, the local branch, which was given the privileged status of a district committee, controlled absolutely everything: the cadres, appointments and administration of policies. Thus the minister de facto lost control over his ministry, officials and even the implementation of policies; he could not be blamed for failures, but he could not gain any credit either. Ministers were moved and sacked, not because they were good or bad administrators; their ministerial office depended on their political standing within the party (or parties).

After the assumption of absolute power in 1948, the Communist Party of Czechoslovakia did not solve the problem of political domination and efficient administration. After 1948, the Communist Party controlled absolutely central government as the expression of its political victory. In 1960, this was put right constitutionally and the Party became the leading force in Czechoslovak society, therefore the absolute ruler. However, the government never got back its powers of decision, nor the professional civil service, and paradoxically Czechoslovakia continued to be governed by a coalition whose policies either failed or were not executed.

CIVIL SERVICE

The disappearance of the professional civil service was one reason for difficulties in central administration. Another reason for difficulties was the continuation of pre-coup practice of appointing politicians as ministers, who, in fact, had become administrative heads. Even the most capable administrators among these politicians would have found it impossible to run central ministries efficiently with the politically-reliable but administratively-unfit officials at their disposal. The Communist Party was not content with controlling absolutely the existing administration; it decided to control practically everything, from the economy to culture. This was well in line with the Soviet model, and the choice of central ministries to achieve control was also typical. However, after 1950, when a whole host of ministries was established, central government and public administration in Czechoslovakia ground to a halt. Gradually, the Communist Party became aware of this administrative collapse and quickly launched a series of reforms. Thus, in 1953, a new ministry of State Control was established whose sole aim was to search for administrative problems and put them right. Significantly the new minister, K. Bacílek, was a former policeman and Minister of State Security, but the ministry failed to improve significantly the state administration, and was dissolved in 1960.

In 1953, the government itself tried to improve its working efficiency. It established a presidium comprising the Premier and his deputies whose function was to be a sort of inner cabinet. It was supposed to run the day-to-day affairs of the government between government sessions (roughly twice a month), co-ordinate the work of various ministries and generally improve administration. Thus, it tried to re-establish the civil service, by requiring educational qualifications from the newly appointed officials. Many workers were sent back to their factories, others moved from administrative tasks to clerical duties. However, the majority of the new men succeeded in gaining educational qualifications (e.g. from the Party High School), and they had to be left in their posts. Needless to say that such half-measures also failed to improve administrative efficiency.

In 1956, the Communist Party launched another reform: the planning and economic management was to be overhauled and a new economic administration introduced. However, the reform carried out between 1958 and 1960 also failed to dislodge the unqualified party officials and achieved nothing significant. In December 1964, the central committee decided on yet another reform: new cadre policies were to be applied to central government and on January 1, 1966, a new system of planning and economic management would come into effect. Even in 1966, the problem of who should exercize power was not resolved; politically reliable technocrats still failed to replace political appointees and the reform would have failed completely, had it not been for the events in 1968. Only in that year did the Communist Party come to the conclusion that, without a professional civil service and administrative restructuring, Czechoslovakia could not be administered in the proper sense of the word.

CENTRAL GOVERNMENT

The program of reform which the Communist Party of Czechoslovakia promulgated in April 1968 stated quite clearly that the existing executive arrangements were unsatisfactory. Thus the government's responsibility to the National Assembly and ministerial responsibility in general were insufficiently clear: "attempts were made to transfer ministerial responsibility to party organs and give up independent decision making. The government is not only the organ (executive) of economic policies. As the supreme organ of executive power it must concern itself as a whole with the entire gamut of political and administrative problems of the state. The government must also concern itself with the rational development of the entire state machinery. In the past, the machinery of state administration had been underestimated; it is imperative that the machinery is run by qualified civil servants, is rationally developed, controlled by democratic means and above all made effective. Past simplifications, such as that national aims can be achieved by ignoring, or even weakening, the administrative apparatus, caused more damage than improvement." Substantial changes were demanded.

Constitutionally, the position of the government, as the chief executive organ, has not changed much since 1920. In the Socialist Constitution of 1960, Communist ideas on central government are outlined above. While the descriptive parts are almost identical with those from the Soviet Constitution of 1936, presidential and parliamentary provisions make Czechoslovak functional arrangements quite different from the Soviet ones. The government is appointed by the President on the recommendation of the National (Federal) Assembly and shares with him the power of appointment of higher civil servants, foreign service officials, university professors and higher army officers. Article 70 (para. 2) states unequivocally that "the government . . . goes about its tasks in narrow co-operation and collaboration with the National Assembly and its organs".

The differences are quite significant and, in the past, they enabled Presidents Gottwald and Novotný, who were also party leaders, to dominate the executive both politically and administratively. As for the National Assembly, there has always been a meaningful co-operation between the executive and legislative, and the two branches of power have had a long and concrete experience of collaboration. The most persuasive demonstration of this is the fact that the President, on the whole, appoints ministers from the National Assembly rather than from the party apparatus. Although this practice has been modified and numerous exceptions made, it is still observed.

The constitutional amendments (Acts 77-1968Sb and 143-1986Sb), passed on October 28, 1968, which transformed Czechoslovakia into a federal republic, did not substantially alter the role of the government. Henceforth Czechoslovakia has, in fact, three governments, one federal and two republican, but their role as chief executive organs remains the same, only their competence is freshly delineated. The federal government's competence comprises (i) foreign affairs; (ii) defense; (iii) federal reserves, and (iv) federal legislation and constitutionalism. The Czech and Slovak governments consist of twelve ministries each, and eleven central administrations. The federal government shares competence with the two republican governments in the departments of (i) Planning; (ii) Finance; (iii) Prices; (iv) Trade; (v) Industry; (vi) Agriculture; (vii) Transport; (viii) Post and Telecommunications; (ix) Science and Technology; (x) Labor, Wages and Social Security; (xi) Normalization; (xii) Internal Order and Security; (xiii) Press and Information. Since January 1, 1969, when the federal constitution came into effect, the structure and competence of government became more complex, but otherwise little different. In the new scheme, the President appoints the federal government on the recommendation of the Federal Assembly; the republican governments are appointed by the Speakers of the Czech and Slovak National Councils which co-operate with the national governments in the close, traditional way.

GOVERNMENT COMPOSITION

When, in February 1948, the Communist Party achieved an absolute majority in the coalition government (13 ministries out of 22), the other political parties were not banned from government: the coalition continued intact. While the Czech Socialist Party and People's Party suffered heavy losses (they each lost a Deputy Premiership), the Social Democrats actually improved their position in the government: they not only held on to the Deputy Premiership (B. Laušman), but also controlled the ministry of Industry (Z. Fierlinger), Social Security (E. Erban) and Food (L. Jankovcová). At this stage, Gottwald still presided over a coalition government composed of politicians (party leaders) whose policies were decided by the government itself and executed by the civil service. After the election in May 1948, and resignation of President Beneš, the government of February 1948 also stood down. Gottwald was elected unanimously President of the Czechoslovak Republic and A. Zápotocký succeeded him as Prime Minister. On June 15, 1948, on the recommendation of the National Assembly, President Gottwald appointed a new government, headed by his old political friend and chairman of the Czechoslovak Central Unions Council, Antonín Zápotocký. It was, once again, a coalition government, but the non-Communist representation decreased still further.

Shortly after the election, the Social Democrats 'joined' the Communist Party and ceased to be represented in the government separately. The Czech Socialists were given the ministries of Post (A. Neuman) and Technology (Professor E. Šlechta), while the People's Party controlled the ministries of Transport (A. Petr) and Health (Reverend J. Plojhar). A lonely Slovak Revival Party member, V. Šrobár, headed the ministry of Law Unification until 1950, when it was dissolved.

Although the Communist Party now controlled the government absolutely, and Premier Zápotocký was second to the party leader Gottwald, the latter took in fact the government firmly into his own hands, creating a kind of presidential regime. In Czechoslovakia, this was not such an unusual arrangement: in the past, during emergencies and crises, Presidents Masaryk and Beneš also established such arrangements. What was more significant, at this stage, was Gottwald's fusion of the presidential and party offices. After 1949, when Gottwald could dispense with the services of the National Assembly, and had time to build up a parallel party apparat to all the administration in the state, he could govern virtually without anyone else. The power of the Prime Minister evaporated and that of the ministers soon went as well.

So far, members of the government were also parliamentary deputies and were appointed by the President as ministers from the National Assembly. By 1950, Gottwald took to making appointments as he pleased: he dismissed General Svoboda as Defense Minister and appointed his Minister of Justice in his stead. Contrary to constitutional usage, he appointed Š. Rais as Minister of Justice, although he was not a member of parliament, and was, in fact, a civil servant from the Presidential Chancellory. Subsequently, Gottwald made many similar appointments, especially to the newly established economic ministries. By then, the government was reduced to the status of the civil service pure and simple, for it had also ceased to make its own policy decisions, which were taken over by party organs (mainly departments of the central committee) and finalized by the President himself.

This new practice of ministerial appointments was strongly disliked, even in the Communist Party, though no one dared to object to it. Party leaders expected ministerial appointments for party loyalty and work. Gottwald, who probably fully appreciated the change of role of the government, refused to appoint his party colleagues to ministerial jobs, and stuck to his decision as long as he lived. Thus in 1949, when he established another ministry, the State Planning Commission, he made his finance minister, Professor J. Dolanský, its first head. At this stage, Dolanský's position within the Communist Party was not particularly strong, but subsequent leaders could not do without his expert knowledge and experience, and he ended up as the most unlikely member of the party presidium under President Novotný. He was replaced in the ministry of Finance by J. Kabeš, whose standing in the party was no greater. Similarly, the minister of Education, Z. Nejedlý, a party presidium member, was replaced by E. Sýkora, without equivalent party standing: the minister of Heavy Industry became J. Maurer; Dolanský was later replaced by J. Pučík, a technocrat rather than a politician.

Gottwald still further reduced the power of the executive by frequent reorganizations. In 1949, after he had created the Central Planning Commission, he transformed the various branches of industry into ministries. In 1950, the ministry of Industry, which up to then had administered all the industries in Czechoslovakia, became the ministry of Heavy Industry (subsequently of Heavy Engineering) and, at the same time, he set up a ministry of Light Industry. (The minister, J. Jonáš, was again more a technocrat than a political leader.) The ministry of Technology, run by the Czech Socialist minister, Professor Šlechta, was dissolved and a new ministry of Building was set up for him. A year later, ministries of Fuel and Energy, Furnaces and Ore Mines, General Engineering, Forests and Wood Industry, as well as Chemical Industries, were established and all went to technocrats rather than politicians-presidium members: L. Kopřiva became the minister of State Security and K. Bacílek minister of State Control. Gottwals added a few ministries to the government in 1952: ministry of Railways (J. Pospíšil) and ministry of Agricultural Purchases (J. Krosnář), but early in 1953, just before his death, he re-organized the government so thoroughly that it came to resemble almost completely the Soviet government. Ministries and state committees (with ministerial status) were created even in fields where there was nothing to administer in Czechoslovakia. Thus the ministry of Universities (L. Štoll) lasted exactly seven months; similarly the ministries of Building Materials (J. Kyselý), State Farms (M. Šmída), Energy (B. Šrámek), Committee for Arts (J. Taufer) and Committee of Cultural Relations with Foreign Countries (J. Urban). Since all these ministries were headed by politicians, it is just possible that Gottwald finally gave way to their pressure. At the time of Gottwald's death, the government of Czechoslovakia consisted of 36 ministries and in size rivaled the Soviet government, although perhaps it was not proportionate to the population and economic wealth of Czechoslovakia.

Despite Gottwald's predilection for technocrats, the steady expansion of the state apparatus (central and regional administration) between 1948–1953 took care of ambitious party leaders, if Gottwald's purges had failed to deal with them. Gottwald dispensed with all the formalities, held no elections, no government presented its program or accounts to the National Assembly, and the ministries were the safest jobs, except for re-shuffles and re-organizations. It was most disconcerting, for example, for such an ambitious leader as J. Ďuriš to find himself without a ministry reflecting his party status, after one of these re-organizations. Still, with Gottwald's death, all this was bound to come to an end, for there was no strong personality left in the Communist Party to carry on.

It took the Communist Party six months to plan its new policies. In September 1953, a whole series of ministries and state committees was dissolved. But the most significant reform was contained in the governmental order 5-1953, by which the work of the government itself was regulated. Until then, at least according to constitutional usage, the government was a collective body which made its decisions at regular (weekly) meetings and controlled their implementation subsequently. In 1953, Soviet constitutional arrangements were copied: the Prime Minister and his deputies formed a presidium (a sort of inner cabinet) which alone had power of decision; it also carried on the business of the government, in between meetings which were now spaced at greater intervals (monthly). This reform was supposed to make the government work really effectively and strengthen the executive considerably. However, the reform failed, for the Czechoslovak politicians were unused to this arrangement and did not know how to work it. The government's powers were strengthened, nevertheless, but for the simple reason that the new President, A. Zápotocký, insisted on being a constitutional figurehead and refused to assume the chairmanship of the Communist Party, thus separating the two powerful positions. Between 1953 and 1957, it seemed that the government would recover its former powers and constitutional position, and more efficient administration of Czechoslovakia would be resumed.

However, even this new system of collective leadership failed to bring about the desired aims. The newly formed government and its ministries continued to act as in the past, refused to accept responsibility and tried to cope with operational problems by hiring more personnel. They succeeded in pushing responsibility for failure from themselves onto the Planning Commission or on the governmental presidium which allegedly made decisions no ministry could implement. It was the old vicious circle again and in 1955 yet another re-organization was ordered (Order 48-1955). Then suddenly, in 1956, many of the reforms of 1955 were canceled and instead new ministries were established. The government reversed its ruling on the established posts in the civil services: civil servants who had required educational qualifications but proved "unsuccessful" were dismissed and the unqualified "political" civil servants were reestablished, provided that they were able to acquire some sort of degree, usually from a party school or institution.

President Zápotocký's virtual resignation from power brought forward the administrative head of the Communist Party, Antonín Novotný. In 1953, he was for some six months deputy Prime Minister, but otherwise his experience was with the party. When, however, in 1957, Zápotocký died, Novotný had himself elected President of Czechoslovakia and once again fused the offices of President and head of the Communist Party. Even such short a term as Deputy Premier convinced Novotný that the executive had to be revived somehow, and he and the party devised several new schemes between 1958 and 1960. Though they were all supposed to simplify central administration, introduce new planning methods in the economy, they invariably had the opposite effect from the intended one. Perhaps as a result of past errors, and certainly as a consequence of administrative malfunctioning, Czechoslovakia was in the grip of an economic recession between 1962 and 1964. In 1965, one more system of planning and administration was devised and passed by the Communist Party. The new system came into effect on January 1, 1966, and was supposed to modernize everything, the economy, administration and planning. It even contained provisions against the misuse of the new methods by local administrators. Though it was too soon to see the final results of this reform, the experiment was not proceeding satisfactorily. The events in 1968 interrupted the reform which was proclaimed insufficient and the subsequent re-organization of central administration and government on federal lines finally ended it.

GOVERNMENT STRUCTURES

Throughout the period 1948–1968, a sustained growth of the administrative machine was recorded. In 1948, Czechoslovakia was administered through its ministries; by 1953, their number rose to 38. Though a number of ministries was abolished after Gottwald's death, the reforms in 1955–56 resurrected many of them—some became state committees, others central administrations. In 1967, after another reform, the government controlled directly the following state committees and central administrations: (i) State Planning Commission; (ii) Commission for Classification of Mineral Resources; (iii) Research Institute of Economic Planning; (iv) State Statistical Office; (v) Slovak Statistical Office; (vi) Research Institute of Control, Evidence and Statistics; (vii) State Commission of Direction and Organization (with the Institute of Management and the Institute of State Administration; (viii) State Commission of Technology (with the Office of Normalization and Measures, Meteorological Office, Institute of Electro Technology, Institute of Engineering, Office of Patents and Inventions, Institute of Radioisotopes, Institute of Material Manipulation, Institute of Accountancy and Automation, Research Institute of Building and Architecture, State Institute of Regional Planning, Institute of Typology, Central Office of Science, Technology and Economic Information, Research Institute of Economics and Development, as well as the Czechoslovak Commission of Atomic Energy); (ix) State Commission of Finance, Prices and Wages, and finally (x) the Central Commission of People's Control.

Each ministry also had several central administrations under its jurisdiction. Thus the ministry of Finance included the Research Institute of Finance, Czechoslovak Commercial Bank, Investment Bank,

Central Office of Property and Currency, State Insurance Office, Central Administration of Savings Banks, Trade Bank, State Bank of Czechoslovakia and the State Mint. Industrial ministries were regular monsters: thus the ministry of Mining, in addition to all the coal mines, administered uranium mines, gas production, iron ore mines, also the Central Office of Geology, Institute of Applied Geophysics, and many other administrations and institutes. The ministry of Transport, for example (established by a parliamentary decree 3 in 1963), administered, apart from all the railways, river shipping and air transport, some 31 other administrations and research establishments. The ministry of Trade which was established in 1945 (presidential decree 1-1945), chiefly to help with the reconstruction of shops, wholesale businesses and also with controlling prices, was by 1967 a super-ministry with 10 research institutes and central administrations, all the shops in Czechoslovakia, as well as tourism, hotels and all the other services. The ministry of foreign trade had the monopoly of exports and controlled 36 export corporations, research institutes, customs and excise, as well as all the chambers of commerce. The ministry of Health, which had also grown considerably since its establishment in 1945, controlled 33 research institutes, 18 spas, as well as the entire pharmaceutical industry, doctors, hospitals, nurses and a supply system. Only the ministry of Education did not seem to have grown out of all proportion: it administered schools and universities adding to its responsibilities only the occasional research institute. In contrast, the ministry of Culture and Information (established by parliamentary presidium decree 1-1967) administered all cultural activity in the country: book publishing, theaters, museums, art galleries, concerts, authors copyright, the press, cultural relations with foreign countries, and also protected nature and churches. Film production and film making, as well as the Czechoslovak Press Agency were included together with broadcasting, television and the Academy of Sciences.

Some traditional ministries, such as the ministry of Foreign Affairs, Internal Affairs, Defense and Justice, after many reforms still retained their structures more or less intact and had not grown excessively. However, a whole series of non-traditional central administrations was established to accomplish specific tasks. In 1954 (governmental decree 20-1954) the Central Mining Office was founded to supervize the implementation of the mining law passed three years later (Act 41-1957Sb). In 1966, the Central Publications Administration came into being (Act 81-1966Sb); it was in fact the central censorship office coordinating the supervision of all the communication media so that "no state, economic and army secrets were published". Other central administrations, such as the Central Commission of Workers' Education, State Commission of Science Degrees, State Population Commission, State Committee of Tourism, etc. were usually attached to various ministries and staffed by them. With the federal arrangements coming into force in 1969, central administration was made even more complex: the two republics are administered by separate governments and federal ministries administer federal affairs. Though certain modifications have been envisaged, the structure of central administration and government in Czechoslovakia still remains as huge, complex and impressive as in the USSR.

DECISION MAKING

Traditionally, Czechoslovakia had a government which met regularly (every week or so), made collective policy decisions which were then implemented by individual departments of state ministries. After the coup d'Etat in 1948, this practice was gradually discontinued, however the Soviet practice of holding joint government and Communist Party presidium meetings (and issuing government and central committee policy statements) has not been imitated and never came into use. During the personality cult period, President Gottwald found it easier to issue instructions from his office to individual ministries, and ultimately came to make all government decisions himself as the leader. After Gottwald's death, Czechoslovakia began to imitate the USSR: government meetings were held after central committee sessions and policy statements were simply re-iterated in more administrative terms. However, the period 1953–58 was rather confused and it is almost impossible to determine how government policies were formulated and how decisions were made.

Only after 1958 did the way the system worked become clear: by this time the Presidency and party leadership were fused again, but Novotný was no Gottwald. Though he used some of the latter's methods, he could not use them all, thus the system was doomed to fail. On January 21, 1958, President Novotný reported to the central committee of the Communist Party of Czechoslovakia on the Communist summit meeting in Moscow. Almost simultaneously, the Czechoslovak government announced its position on the atom free zone in Central Europe, a matter discussed both in Moscow and in the Central Committee. At another meeting of the central committee, on February 27 and 28, 1958, new arrangements for finance, planning in industry, and building, as well as the economic effects of investments were discussed. On March 16, 1958, the government announced its own plans for a new organization of industry which were coming into force on April 1, 1958: this shows quite conclusively that the re-organization was prepared and sanctioned by the Communist Party (or better still by the First Secretary and President). On June 16, 1958, the central committee announced its own measures for increased efficiency of the local economy; the government responded by announcing the same concrete measures on July 11. It also ordered improvements in the organization of the coming harvest with which the central committee had not dealt. Between June 19 and 22, 1958, the 11th Congress of the Communist Party of Czechoslovakia took place; it discussed the new Five Year Plan and approved the concrete proposals laid before it by the presidium. On August 1st, 1958, the government made public new targets for the Five Year Plan, and also approved organizational changes discussed by the Congress. It is not at all clear who had prepared the economic plan; but it is obvious that the Congress of the Communist Party had made final decisions and the government simply undertook to execute the plan.

In 1959, this pattern of decision making became a regular feature of the government's work. On March 7, 1959, the central committee approved an increase in child allowances, a decrease in shop prices, increase in pensions and a cut in working hours. Exactly the same announcements were made by the government on the same day giving them legal force. However, the April session of the central committee in 1959 was not followed by identical government announcements: the new agricultural purchase system, as well as the new prices of agricultural produce, were dealt with by the government in August, September and October 1959. At last concrete measures on agricultural purchases and prices were taken by the government itself. The Five Year Plan, which the central committee discussed both in April and September 1959, was also dealt with by the government in July and December 1959. The evident lag of government measures behind the central committee's decisions was undoubtedly due to the difficulty of translating general policies into administrative terms.

In 1960, the government announced its budget on February 18, long before the session of the central committee, which took place in April. This must have been due to the party's preoccupation with a new constitution. On the other hand, the government was still clearing up the backlog of party decisions from 1959: it announced reforms of collective farms, improvements in agricultural machinery as well as reduction of shop prices, together with free school books and other social measures. The April session of the central committee discussed the new constitution and increased the powers of local government. It probably also approved a general amnesty—convicted party leaders, Dr. Husák among them, were finally released from prisons and concentration camps—which the President proclaimed on May 9, 1960.

In June 1960, the government proclaimed the reform of local government whose powers, in particular the financial ones, were considerably increased, and made the reform effective henceforth. It is obvious that it accepted the project of the reform from the Communist Party. In July 1960, in addition to the constitution, the central committee dealt with the Five Year Plan, agriculture and probably also the composition of the new government which was appointed after the general election. Premier Široký continued in office and only very few changes were made, none of them politically significant. The new government dealt with the economy and the plan on August 7, 1960. In October 1960, the government implemented two measures previously decided upon by the central committee: university appointments and finance were newly regulated. In addition, wages in the building industry were increased and a new way of financing house building was devised. Perhaps a little paradoxically, on October 23, 1960 the recently strengthened local government saw some of the local taxes abolished. The government took no action, not even in 1961, on central committee decisions arrived at in December 1960; another re-organization of the chemical industry was announced together with the "renovation" of socialist legality.

In 1961, perhaps surprisingly, it was the turn of the central committee to react to government plans and measures rather than anticipating them. In February 1961, the central committee dealt with such blanket subjects as agriculture, building and railways; no concrete decisions were made. On the other hand, in June 1961, the government announced an increased building program and improvements in agricultural production. The June session of the central committee backed up these measures, by ordering the district administration and district party committees to help directly in the villages. In September 1961, the party tried again to buttress the government measures, announcing the formation of a new university, as well as new arrangements for part-time students. Subsequently, the central committee announced its intentions of making national education a truly Communist one; it also decided to increase party propaganda in educational establishments. At the November session the central committee dealt with youth as a whole, and in particular endorsed government measures concerning the universities.

In 1962, the Communist Party devoted most of its attention to the preparation of the crucial 12th Congress, and only one session, in February, was devoted to problems in the economy and agriculture. In contrast, the government appeared very busy running the economy and agriculture; in January 1962, it announced additional measures for the improvement of agricultural production. In February, new labor norms came into effect. And preventative measures against mining accidents were taken. The film industry was re-organized, agricultural purchases were modified and a new State Committee for Development was set up. In March 1962, additional measures were taken to organize agricultural work more effectively and, in June 1962, concrete plans for dealing with the harvest were announced. Previously the government had increased collective farmers' social security and pensions and it was no surprise that the Five Year Plan was fulfilled satisfactorily. In July 1962, the government dealt with transport problems and in August with the harvest as well as public health. In September 1962, the government approved the planning targets and prepared the budget which were then discussed and passed in the National Assembly.

The 12th Congress of the Communist Party of Czechoslovakia was a turning point, which meant a break with many past practices. The relations between the central committee and the government were newly regulated: so far apparently, party organs had been supplanting central administration and, as a consequence, no one was willing to make decisions and accept responsibility for them. Failures of, and deficiency in, central administration were attributed to the Communist Party and this could not continue. The presidium decided on a radical change: new men were needed to carry out new policies. In a major re-shuffle, Premier V. Široký, together with a number of political ministers (Ďuriš, Krosnář, Kahuda, but also Štrougal), were dismissed and the new government under the youthful J. Lenárt introduced new ways of administration. The government was to receive from the Communist Party only long-term and general instructions, and even these directives were to be prepared by central committee commissions especially established for the purpose. The commissions were to work out "conceptual problems" (economic, agricultural, ideological, etc.), have them approved by the central committee, which would then pass them on to the government for implementation. It was also suggested that new statutes should be worked out for individual ministries, so that they also could carry out their administrative tasks in a new way. To improve administration still further, it was suggested that individual responsibility be re-introduced into administrative work, structures streamlined and personnel cut.

Henceforth, apart from annual budgets and some urgent procla-
mations (e.g. "save electricity"), no publicity was given to joint central
committee and government meetings and decisions. In 1964, the
central committee dealt with economic development and living standards: on February 7, the government announced measures concerning
both. In April 1964, the government presented its budget, while the
central committee dealt with cultural matters. In 1966, there was only
one joint party-government statement and it concerned the Communist
Summit Meeting at Bucharest. In 1967, there were no joint statements
at all, while the central committee discussed a whole gamut of general
problems: youth, agriculture, local government, economic plan and
balance, living standards, general election in 1968, etc. It is probable
that the party in-fighting and struggle for the leadership left the
government relatively free to tackle national problems and administer
the country. All the same, in April 1968, Premier Lenárt was dismissed
and accused of carrying out blindly party directives instead of governing and administering Czechoslovakia.

In 1968, in the program of action, new working arrangements
between the Communist Party and the government were established.
Although the party presidium and central committee still reserved
for themselves the right to proclaim policies, as a guidance for the
government, the executive was otherwise be left free to govern and
administer the country. The Communist Party, moreover, was only
issue general policy statements, prepared after exhaustive consultations
with party commissions and the National Front, which includes other
political parties as well as 'interest' groups. It is clear that the
government of Czechoslovakia was firmly re-established; however,
before these new arrangements could be properly tested, Czechoslovakia was occupied by the armies of the Warsaw Pact, and it seems
that after 1969 it reverted to the old arrangements of sporadic party
intervention.

MINISTRY OF DEFENSE: A CASE STUDY

If in the past twenty years the central government was treated in
such an untraditional manner and was greatly reduced in its constitutional standing and power, individual ministries did not fare dif-
ferently. Since, however, the Presidents and party leaders could not
dominate them as easily as the government as a whole, they often
succeeded in reversing the downgrading trend and were able to return
to the pre-1948 structural and functional arrangements. The Ministry

of Defense is perhaps the best example of this process. After all, Czechoslovakia accumulated long experience and a sound administrative tradition in the defense field. After 1918, the French mission modified in some respects the army organization inherited from the Habsburg Monarchy, but overall administrative arrangements were left untouched. A politician ran the Ministry of Defense by means of ministerial departments and the general staff; an inter-ministerial council proved particularly effective with procurement policies and, as a result, the Czechoslovak army was the best equipped force in Central Europe and at a reasonable cost.

In 1945, when Czechoslovakia was re-established, the ministry of Defense was also rebuilt in the traditional way, despite the fact that the armies and air forces were heterogenous and organized in all sorts of ways (British and Soviet chiefly). The Minister of Defense, General L. Svoboda, who had fought in the USSR and had also close contacts with Czechoslovak Communist leaders, was responsible for the decision to rebuild the old system. Instead of the Soviet military councils, he re-formed the old ministerial departments: the 1st administered general military affairs, the 3rd was for economic administration and the 5th looked after the air force, while the 6th was concerned with army health. The General Staff also retained its traditional five sections: 1st organization; 2nd (deuxieme bureau) intelligence; 3rd operations. In 1945, on joining the government of Czechoslovakia, the Communist Party insisted on the establishment of two new departments, which it held under its own strict supervision. The department of Education and Enlightenment might have been thought as Branch B of the old system, but in fact it was a direct imitation of the Soviet political system. Major (later Lieutenant General), J. Procházka, who was put in charge of this department, was an experienced Communist Party leader, who knew that this department could neutralize the army, if it became involved in political struggle. The other new department of counter-espionage (HSOZ) was headed by Major B. Reicin, another Communist, and was to be used to destroy the army, if it actually acted against the Communist Party. With these two "insurance" departments under its control, the Communist Party permitted the re-building of the ministry, the inter-ministerial military council, supreme council of state defense and the army consultative council.

After the coup d'Etat in 1948, the Communist Party did not think it necessary to treat the ministry of Defense harshly. The minister of Defense finally joined the Communist Party and a few officers were purged for their pronounced anti-Communist views. Until 1950,

General Svoboda succeeded in keeping both the ministry and the army intact and did not require Soviet military advisors. He even dared to suggest in the government that Czechoslovakia should purchase military equipment in the West, since it could not obtain it from the USSR. But in 1950, President Gottwald decided on a complete re-organization of the ministry and army and appointed his son-in-law, Dr. A. Čepička, to carry it out. The new minister of Defense immediately purged the ministry and the army of Svoboda's officers and staff and began the re-organization: the Czechoslovak army had to be transformed into a complete imitation of the Soviet army in both training and equipment and he called for Soviet advisors to help him. The ministry was to be re-organized as well, and here he needed Soviet advisors. Čepička abolished the supreme council of state defense in 1950 and in 1951 the army consultative council. In their stead, he set up something unique, neither Soviet nor Czechoslovak, the Military Council.

The Military Council was responsible for all defense matters and began to meet once a month. Čepička acted as chairman, his two deputy defense ministers, General Laštovička (a journalist by profession) and General Hruška responsible for political education, were members of the council as well as General Procházka, former Politruk, now Chief of Staff, and ministerial secretary (at first Colonel J. Strašil and, subsequently, Colonel J. Šejna, who sought political asylum in the West in 1968). From the beginning, an equivalent number of Soviet advisors attended the council meetings and undoubtedly dispensed advice. After 1954, the Soviet advisors attended the meetings as visitors, and in 1956 the council was wound up and replaced by the traditional army consultative council. However, apart from this innovation Čepička succeeded only in dis-organizing the army which was completely transformed. The Political Administration (formerly a section of the general staff) was built up and became the department of the central committee of the Communist Party. Its head was one of the deputy defense ministers and member of the central committee. In 1956, Čepička was dismissed and his successor, General B. Lomský started the long haul of re-establishing the ministry and the army. Thus, his deputy ministers were in fact in charge of the old departments and the General Staff. The head of the Political Administration remained deputy defense minister, so that the military had him under better control. By 1968, General Lomský made such good progress in re-establishing his ministry and the army that no great changes were necessary to make the ministry acceptable to the new leaders. Though Lomský was also dismissed for political reasons (apparently he was implicated in a plan to use the army in support of President Novotný), the only change carried out in 1968 was the creation of the Council of State Defense, which in many ways resembles the old Supreme Council of State Defense. Thus, although the Czechoslovak army in training, discipline and equipment, is identical with the Soviet army (and the armies of the Warsaw Pact), in the administration of defense Czechoslovakia is back to traditional arrangements.

The ministry of defense's development is not unique; other ministries went through disruptive experiences only to return to the traditional way of organizing things. In 1951, a new Ministry of National Security was set up to cope with security; immediately after Gottwald's death it was abolished and the Ministry of the Interior resumed its responsibility for security (2nd department). After experiments, the administration of education, science and culture in Czechoslovakia came under the traditional ministries of Education (with science and research included) and Culture. Even in the case of industrial ministries, where there is no tradition, the tendency is to act as top co-ordinating bodies rather than rigid, centralized bureaucracies. However, it is quite clear that the Communist way of running the government and ministries impaired their effectiveness and efficiency. Similarly to the USSR, it was not an administration, but an uncontrolled, self-seeking bureaucratic apparat.

9

THE JUDICIAL SYSTEM

The organization of the judiciary in Czechoslovakia was inherited from Austria-Hungary. Even to-day laws dating back from the 19th century, when there were two separate national entities, the Czech provinces and Slovakia and two different legal systems, are on the Statute book. The Slovak judiciary was based on the Hungarian model, developed after 1867, while the Czech judicial arrangements were modeled on the Austrian pattern: district courts on Act 59, 1868, and the system as such on Act 217, 1896. The Habsburg Monarchy, which was a Rechtstaat, and in Czechoslovakia also, the judiciary, was a separate power which, apart from administering laws, also acted as arbiter between the legislative and the executive. Similarly to its functions, its structure was complex and went back to 1896 (Act No. 217). Two administrative institutions (Nos. 10 and 81) ordering the internal organization and agenda of the courts dated back to 1853. After 1918, only one minor adjustment to the inherited structures was enacted: a new Supreme Court had to be established for the Republic (Act 5). (In addition, in 1919, criminal tribunals were established (Act 451) and in 1932 an administrative instruction (No. 162) regulated the official apparel of the judges.) Otherwise all was left unchanged. The Constitution of Czechoslovakia, passed in 1920, took over the Austrian model (paras. 94–105) almost without any alteration, while in Slovakia the Hungarian judicial arrangements remained in force. Between 1918–1939, the Czechoslovak National Assembly passed only two amendments which affected the judiciary system: in 1923, Act 51, which created a new State Court, to try security and anti-state crimes, and in 1928, Act 201, which attempted to harmonize the Czech and Slovak judicial system. Throughout the first republic (1919–1939) this judicial system proved efficient, and it was no surprise that the independent Slovak state passed a special law (Act 112) in 1942 which added to the Slovak system features from the Czechoslovak one. During the war, 1939–45, there was no rule of law in the Czech and ultimately Slovak provinces, and in 1945 Czechoslovakia had to start from scratch re-building its judiciary. In 1945, the presidential decree, No. 79, resuscitated the old system, i.e. the one that existed on September 29, 1938, (before the Munich diktat destroyed Czechoslovakia). The Czechoslovak government also dealt with the re-building of the judiciary system in its statement of policies (April 5, 1945, chapter 1) in which it proclaimed that it would punish German and Hungarian occupiers and their collaborators. This meant that new courts would have to be created to try such cases.

Some ten types of supreme courts had been in existence in Czechoslovakia before 1948: (i) the Supreme Administrative Court in Prague gave judgements in conflicts between the administration and individuals or groups, or between administrations; (ii) the Electoral Court was competent to deal with electoral matters and problems; (iii) the Patent Court; (iv) the Constitutional Court which interpreted the Constitution; (v) the Supreme Court for criminal matters; (vi) the Procuracy General which prosecuted; (vii) the State Court which judged security cases; (viii) the Supreme Finance Court, and (x) the General Military Procuracy which both dealt with military offences by military offenders.

In addition, each province had its supreme provincial court (the Bohemian in Prague, the Moravian in Brno, the Slovak in Bratislava, etc.). These provincial (zemské soudy) courts were subdivided into criminal and civil courts and in Bohemia even into commercial courts. The whole country was covered by district courts in each administrative district and there was a network of regional courts uniting several district courts. The Procuracy's network was on the regional level and it supervized prisons as well. Thus, in 1945 Czechoslovakia reverted to three types of court: (i) civil courts (ordinary, extraordinary and arbitration tribunals); (ii) criminal courts (which could either be jury tribunals or court martial), and (iii) the State Court, as well as the Kmet courts (which dealt with "public" offences such as libel, etc.). Administrative tribunals such as the Supreme Administrative Court, Constitutional Courts, and the Electoral Courts were also re-established. All judges sitting on these courts were professional men appointed either by the President or the government. The jury tribunals consisted of 12 men juries and three judges: the jury decided the question of guilt and the judges decided the measure of punishment. However, the reforms effected in 1945 and 1946 defined afresh the powers of the reconstituted courts and, as a result, the post-war system was certainly not identical with the pre-war system.

In 1945, the President issued Decree No. 16 (the Retribution Decree) which created in regional courts the so-called peoples's tribunals which were to try German and Hungarian occupiers and their collaborators. There existed also people's tribunals on the district and local levels and they tried cases on these levels. In Slovakia, the Slovak Nation's Council Instruction established these tribunals and in both cases they were certainly points of departure from the traditional way of administering justice. These people's tribunals consisted of five to eleven members, of whom only the chairman was a professional judge appointed by the President. The four to eleven people's judges were appointed by the government and were selected from the jury lists; on the district or local levels, they were appointed by district or local councils on the suggestion of political parties. Occupiers and collaborators of national importance were tried by another special and newly created tribunal, the National Court (Presidential Degree, No. 17). The Slovak National Court tried the former President of Slovakia, its government and other collaborating leaders; the Czech one tried corresponding collaborators from the Czech provinces. Both National Courts consisted of seven-men tribunals whose chairman was invariably a professional judge appointed by the President, while the "national" judges were appointed by the government from the lists of party politicians who had proportionate representation on these tribunals. The fact that the district and local people's tribunals could be presided over by unqualified citizens and that people's judges at all levels were not jury men but were instrumental in punishing the accused was the most important innovation in the Czechosloval judical system. With the simplification of procedures at these retribution tribunals, Czechoslovakia had a first taste of this new extraordinary justice: many sentences passed in 1945–46 proved extremely severe and only in 1947 did the "retribution" ardour begin to cool off. Despite the novelty of the system, after the Communist coup on February 1948, the Communist Party decided to destroy it as it was apparently bourgeois in character.

The systematic destruction of the judiciary system started immediately after the Communist coup with the purge of the Ministry of Justice and courts at all levels. In February 1948, the minister responsible for this department, Dr. Drtina tried unsuccessfully to commit suicide, and was replaced by another lawyer, Dr. Čepička, who was Premier Gottwald's son-in-law, as well as an unbalanced politican suffering from prolonged imprisonment during World War II in the Nazi concentration camp of Oswienczyn. Convinced of the utter wickedness of bourgeois justice, Čepička became the great destroyer and creator of Socialist justice.

The new Constitution which came into force in May 1948, already simplified the judicial system and pointed out the way it would go. It abolished all but one supreme court; the one left in existence was to judge criminal cases. Obviously the electoral and constitutional courts proved superfluous for the new system, but the others were to be missed. The national assembly then passed two acts, No. 319 and 320, which completely "re-organized" the judiciary. Act 319 "democratized" the judiciary; only 4.7% of the judges were of working-class origin and therefore they were all dismissed and replaced by people's judges, ideologically reliable factory workers. This was a remedial, immediate measure, but for the future the Communist Party picked some 3,000 factory workers who were admitted without any academic qualifications to the Faculty of Law at Charles University in Prague and in 18 months were rushed through legal courses which normally took university students five years to complete. Even while studying these extraordinary students practised as professional judges, and on graduation, rather superfluously, they were appointed to the positions which they had occupied previously. Act 319 also contained provisions for the people's judges (again untrained, hand-picked workers) who joined the "professional" judges in court. Subsequently Act 25-1949 fixed the renumeration of these new type judges and Act 267 put a legal seal on the system.

SECURITY ORGANIZATIONS IN CZECHOSLOVAKIA 1948–1968

Prior to the Communist coup, there were two Czechoslovak security organizations: (i) the State Security (StB) which dealt with political (subversion, sabotage) security, and (ii) the HIS section of the General Staff which dealt with military security (espionage, counter-espionage). Both organizations were formed in 1945 and were under the control of the Ministry of the Interior and under close scrutiny from the Ministry of Defense and the military sector sub-committees of the Czechoslovak Parliament which also supervized and checked the activity of the Ministries themselves. The State Security organization was headed by A. Závodský; General Reicin was responsible for the military HIS section.

Before the Communist coup, the most notorious case that the State Security uncovered was the "conspiracy against republic" within the Slovak Democratic Party secretariat in 1947 (Dr. Kempný, Dr. Bugár); the military service scored a success in 'uncovering' the Czechoslovak officers espionage affair at Most in 1948. Judicially both affairs remain obscure to this day, for the accused were neither tried nor sentenced in the legal sense, but the political consequences of these cases were far-reaching. Thus the one caused a political reshuffle in the Slovak board of Commissioners (Sbor poverenikov), as a result of which the Slovak Democratic Party lost its control over that body. The other case caused a crisis within the Czech police force and it became a cause célèbre bringing about the February coup d'Etat.

It is fair to say that while the Czech Communist Party could easily paralyze the security organizations through its members placed in these bodies, it did not control them and, above all, could not rely on them to carry out party orders. The Minister of the Interior, Václav Nosek, was a veteran Communist who tried hard to control the security services, but his control was far from complete. Moreover, many of the regional and district security departments (which were in charge of security on these levels) were in the hands of non-Communists. In turn non-Communists could paralyze security operations, ordered by Communist members of the Communist ministry, As it happened, neither side made use of the security organizations during the coup, but immediately after it the Communists re-organized the service in order to use it against the defeated non-Communists.

The overwhelming success of the coup d'Etat left many Czech Communists astounded. Their opponents simply fled the country or joined them, i.e. became collaborators. It was only in the second half of 1948 that the first attempts at a "come-back" were staged: in July 1948, it was the Sokol (gymnastic display) Festival and in September the funeral of Prsident Beneš. These were allegedly the first attempts at a mass counter-coup, and while the Czech Communist leaders were certainly piqued by these demonstrations, they did not take them too seriously. Internally, the Communist leadership felt quite secure despite many successful escapes from the country by non-Communist politicians, army officers and security men (or possibly because of them). However, in June 1948, Jugoslavia was declared 'deviationist,' and expelled from the Cominform. At the same time, Gottwald met Stalin in the Crimea and discussed with him the political development in Czechoslovakia. Stalin told Gottwald that he was still far from the complete victory he imagined. Real work would only start now: "with the development of socialism the class struggle would inevitably intensify."

On his return, Gottwald immediately took steps to implement Stalin's vague wishes. At first it was thought that Stalin could be appeased by energetic measures and liquidations of the defeated opponents. The new, docile parliament passed a repressive law, Act No. 213, on August 9, 1948. Sixteen days later, Act No. 247 legally established forced labor camps which were to be filled by the purged opponents. The new Minister of Justice, Gottwald's son-in-law, saw to it personally that the tribunals took full advantage of these new laws. Within a month, a whole series of trials was staged; on September 2, 1948, Professor Krajina and his group were tried and liquidated (the Professor, however, succeeded in escaping from Czechoslovakia and now teaches biology in Canada). On September 3, Captain Bláha and Majors Časek and Němec were sentenced heavily for endangering the people's democratic regime. Twenty-five other officers, among whom General Žák, Major Gregor, Captains Němeček and Tauchman followed soon after. On September 17, regional courts dealt with their quotas of people's democratic enemies, but there were no death sentences yet.

In November 1948, the central committee of the Communist Party dealt with Stalin's intensified class struggle suggestions and its conclusions bode ill for the frightened opponents: while in February 1948 they were decisively defeated, now they had to be destroyed whether they still wanted to oppose the Communist Party or not. But for these new tasks the security organizations had to be re-organized, for the existing ones could not be trusted. Thus, all the non-Communists were purged and either dismissed or imprisoned. Nevertheless, only few specialists were retained, while reliable party leaders became district or regional security chiefs. The rank and file of the re-organized services was selected from the workers' militia, whose only qualification for the new jobs was a ruthless loyalty to the Communist leadership. The Minister of the Interior lost control of the new body, which now came under the direct supervision of the party presidium and especially its two leading members, Gottwald and Zápotocký. The re-organization also put a final stop to any legal basis or control of the security organizations. The ministry and the government as a whole not only lost control over them, but henceforth were not even informed of their activity. Until the creation of the Ministry of Security in 1950, the services were run on a practially private basis by the Chairman of the Communist Party, K. Gottwald, through officials of the central committee and the Politburo secretariat of the Communist Party.

After the coup, many security organizations at all levels were run by ad hoc personnel: at district, regional and central levels, security fives formed themselves, consisting of the 1st Communist Party secretary, security secretary, commander of the security police, commander of the uniformed police and state security administrator. This spontaneous arrangement had many advantages and disadvantages; one of the latter was that it was hierarchically controlable from the central committee. The political element was in control and in a sense guaranteed that the security organs would not run amok. But after the reorganization only the central five (pětka) a purely political and executive body survived; its chairman was R. Slánský, the general secretary and the other members were J. Veselý (executive secret police), L. Kopřiva and A. Čepička as political representatives.

One of the first acts of the central security five was to abolish the regional and district fives, leaving only the security command in charge. Thus, at all levels purely executive officers were left acting on orders from the central five. But the re-organization also diminished the presidium's control. Paradoxically, it ceased to deal with security matters and only heard reports from the security five. The central five were thus authorized to order arrests, conduct investigations prior to arrests and examine the arrested. Only arrests of important Communist politicians had to be approved by Gottwald and his secretariat. From the beginning, Gottwald had an uneasy feeling that the security services could get out of hand. He, therefore, insisted on creating a party body, which would have permanent supervision over them, and the Control Party Commission was put in charge of security matters and investigations. Though the recommendation was accepted and J. Taussigová became the watchdog of the commission in security matters, this provision proved quite insufficient. Slánský and Kopřiva, apart from serving on the Central Security Five, were also members of the presidium and only political suicides would dare to investigate or even doubt their word. In 1950 Taussigova dared inopportunely to claim that there existed a Zionist plot in the Carlsbad regional party, and was promptly removed from office by Slánský, who, as a Jew, was the obvious target of this move. Had she waited another year, she probably would have been on safe ground. Šváb and Čepička, the other members of the Security Five were also in impregnable positions: the former was the brother of M. Švermová, presidium member, and the latter was Gottwald's son-in-law. Only J. Veselý, a professional, was vulnerable and indeed he disappeared without a trace, undoubtedly after he had done his damage.

It is true that, while politically the Central Security Five was well equipped for its tasks, to repress the class enemy, professionally it was not very skilled or experienced. Nonetheless, it could fall back on the old tricks of the trade, i.e. provocation, forgeries and forced confessions. Old security experts helped in the first few cases. Thus, in May 1949, they used an agent provocateur to arrest and sentence a "resistance group" consisting of officers led by General Kutlvašr, hero of the Prague uprising in 1945. The agent provocateur then had to be murdered as well. Many similar cases, and apparent lack of success with "really dangerous opponents", forced Gottwald to turn to Stalin with a request for special security advisors. These specialists were called in, not only to help the Czechs uncover and liquidate class enemies, but also to catch enemies within the party itself. In October 1949, two generals of the Soviet Security Police, Makarov and Likhachev took up their appointments in Prague and shortly afterwards all the security sections of the Ministry of Security had Soviet advisors.

Needless to say, the central security five was an illegal and ad hoc body which formed itself without any proper authority. However, it was only in 1950 that Gottwald suddenly decided to "legalize" his security arrangements, by creating a new Ministry of Security. L. Kopřiva, one of the five, became the minister and Šváb his deputy. In the meantime, the security situation in Czechoslovakia deteriorated to such an extent, that the Soviet advisors began their struggle against the enemy within the party. Despite the new Ministry of Security, Gottwald continued to use the special party security commission, to investigate security matters, especially those concerning party members and party leaders. Thus, in his party capacity, Šváb investigated nationalist conspiracies in Slovakia, while B. Kohler, J. Frank, A. Baramová and F. Prachář investigated the Brno affair, which later was turned into an anti-party conspiracy, in which R. Slánský and practically everybody in the party leadership concerned with security was implicated.

The repression of the anti-Communist opposition also continued; during the 1950 thousands of non-communist politicians were arrested and "passed" through the re-organized security machine. The results were momentous: in June 1950, after a show trial, the state tribunal sentenced four of the accused (among them a woman, Dr. Horáková) to death and many others to centuries of imprisonment. Significantly, politicians of all the non-Communist parties only were on trial, among them friends of the ruling party leaders—this was in fact the first major public trial of the non-Communists. Many other trials followed, the two most important ones were those of the Prague and Brno opposition groups, during which death sentences were pronounced. Nonetheless, these were political trials intended to intimidate and destory Communist opponents. So far, no one dared to subject the ruling party to a purge comparable to that in the USSR in 1937–38 or 1947–48. When the Soviet advisor, Boyarsky, tried to implicate several leading party members in the web of investigation of the defeated opponents, Gottwald put his foot down quite resolutely and had the advisor recalled to Moscow.

It is probable that the political committee and Gottwald himself began to realize that the arrests, investigations, interrogations and public trials of their opponents would soon extend to the Communist Party and its leadership and they made an attempt at stemming this security avalanche. V. Kopřiva, the Minister of Security, later declared that, after attending international Communist conferences on intraparty purges, he himself became afraid for his own skin. As an expert, he clearly realized that the Soviet advisors and their Czechoslovak helpers were uncontrollable and completely out of hand: for him security work could no longer foster a political career but became a danger to it. In 1951, Gottwald, probably on Kopřiva's advice, made a last effort at imposing his will on the security organs and, in a surprise move, had most of the personnel of the proliferating and illegal apparatus arrested. Šváb, Pavel, Bartík, Závodský and all the section chiefs for national security were taken into custody, as they were leaving a meeting convoked by the politburo member, Kopřiva. Most of them were massacred and only a few survived to tell the tale; one of them, J. Pavel, was destined to play the exalted role of Minister of the Interior in 1968.

But this massive and bloody purge of the security services failed to solve the ills and dangers of the Czechoslovak Communist Party. Soon Soviet advisors, in particular Generals Makarov and Likhachev, became quite hysterical about subversive elements in the Communist Party itself and, aided by such interrogators as A. Prchal, D. Doubek, K. Košťál and V. Kohoutek, obtained confessions incriminating members of the top party leadership. While persecutions of opponents continued unabated, the security apparatus turned to the party as well and, after producing "proofs", Gottwald and the politburo gave permission for top arrests.

In fact, the purge of the security organs only provided for its streamlining. The newly appointed security agents were "specially" selected: most of them had no qualifications for the appointment, but were loyal party members willing to obey orders from fanatical workers militia members. In addition, the judiciary was properly purged and new judges and magistrates were appointed. Already in 1948, there was a provision in law 323 that in individual cases judges and magistrates could be appointed without proper educational qualifications. By 1952, the Minister of Justice had no need of this provision. In December 1952, 225 "special" lawyers graduated from the Faculty of Law, Prague University. They were all specially selected Communists without previous educational qualifications; with brand new degrees they were prepared to administer revolutionary justice.

Throughout 1952 the party leaders in Czechoslovakia were in a state of excitement. After the mass arrests in 1951, the purge was snowballing into a catastrophe and no one knew whose turn it would be next. Central committee members, ministers, civil servants, security agents, economists, generals and intellectuals were slowly pulled in, each group yielding a given number, as if quotas had been fixed in advance. Then in November 1952, the greatest political trial was staged in which the Secretary-General of the Party, R. Slánský, Foreign Minister V. Clementis and many others were destroyed. It is true that they all had bent the very law which now liquidated them, but the circumstances of their demise were so sordid and such a travesty of justice—the sentences were based on confessions obtained after torture—that even several party leaders were appalled. L. Kopřiva, Minister of Security, retired shortly afterwards; in 1968, he declared that he could not face such terrible justice, let alone feel responsible for it. He also added that his own security agents were after his blood, too.

Throughout 1952–53, security agents were busy clearing up the party purges, and while, following on Stalin's death, the wave of party arrests relented, this was not because there were no people to be purged, but rather it was a necessary halt to clear up the previous mass arrests. In February 1953 the most ruthless interrogators Prchal, Doubek, Košťál and Kohoutek received high decorations for their performance. Only in 1954 were the last of the people arrested in the purges sentenced (Outrata, Taussigová, etc.) and a new look was taken at the security organization.

In December 1953, all the satellite countries were in receipt of a circular letter from the Soviet party leadership in which "Beria and his gang" were blamed for excesses in the security services. Czechoslovakia also had a new Minister of Security, R. Barák. On taking over from his predecessor, J. Bacílek, Barák was told that his "machine (Ministry) is simply magnificient; it runs alone and no care is needed; even if the Minister tried to halt it, he would not succeed". However, Barák refused to become such as passive minister; he obviously thought that he would build his career on the security machine, even if paradoxically it meant destroying it. Nonetheless, it took him almost two years to initiate an investigation of excesses, which would lead to the weakening of the dangerous instrument under his control. In January 1955, on A. Novotný's proposal, Barák, Ineman, Košťál, Litera and Švach formed a commission to investigate the abuse of power by security organs. Shortly afterwards, Košťál had to be dismissed, for it transpired that he had participated in the very abuses under investigation. The upshot of this investigation was limited, only a few investigators were dismissed and arrested (Doubek, Kohoutek); the sentences of Smrkovský, Pavel, Goldstücker, London and others were revized. On April 23, 1956, the politburo accepted the Commission's report, but decided to do nothing about it: political upheavals within the Communist orbit were the excuse for inactivity.

After Stalin's death, the Czechoslovak Communist Party and its leaders were in a difficult position concerning the security services. To start with, it was impossible to take action against them, for they were needed. In June–July 1955, large scale mutinies occurred in concentration camps in the Jáchymov and Příbram areas, and the security forces proved invaluable in restoring the situation. These camps were vital to the national economy, for prisoners worked in uranium mines, and disruption of production would have fatal consequences. In August 1955, hunger strikes and mutinies occurred in one of the largest jail in the country at Leopoldov. Again the security police cracked up this dangerous insurrection. At the same time, however, the party was quite unwilling to use the security organs against the party itself: hence the tendency to exclude security experts at least from factional conflicts within the party. Thus in 1953, and again in 1956 and 1961, the so-called Yugoslav groups, i.e. Czechoslovak party members who saw advantages in the Yugoslav system and advocated its adoption, were expelled from the party and hunted down in the social sense—since they were practically all intellectuals they had to do manual work for decades—but were not arrested, or imprisoned. The central committee security department (section 8) dealt with these cases, (Koucký, Pastyřík, Mamula, Kudrna) thus shortcircuiting the security police. But security police powers still remained wide and in 1957, when A. Novotný finally became the absolute leader and Gottwald's successor, he resolutely refused to curtail them any further, thus making it clear that he would make use of them, if special circumstances required it.

In 1956, R. Barák, the Minister of the Interior, headed the 2nd Commission investigating excesses of the security organs in the party. In 1957, the security policemen who had committed crimes against "humanity", i.e. torture, were finally arrested, tried and sentenced to long terms of imprisonment. However, investigators and even assassins who practiced their crude arts on non-Communists were either reprimanded and kept on, or only dismissed from the service: the security apparat remained intact, apart from notorious culprits.

The new leader, Novotný, obviously intended to fall back on this efficient power instrument, if necessary. Curiously enough he now decided to use the security police against his own police chief, Barák, who went round asking embarrassing questions and reporting to the politburo on past security mistakes. In September 1958, Barák was persuaded that no revision of trials that had taken place during the purges was necessary, but by raising this explosive affair he condemned himself. Novotný had this busybody discredited by planting forged evidence on him; he arrested the minister personally, and in 1962 had him sentenced to 15 years forced labor.

It is true that in 1963 the party's "Kolder Commission" rehabilitated the majority of those purged in the 1950s, but it was obvious also that President Novotný was most unwilling to dismantle the security police in the same way as the other Communist countries. He considered it as his personal power instrument, to be kept in reserve for an emergency. Thus, he continued to protect this agency which carried on its nefarious activity to the last day of the Novotný era. It was allowed to stage several mass trials of non-Communists and party members in the 1960s; the former were usually accused of sedition or subversive activity, while the latter were tried for sabotage and subversion. (However, purely political disagreements within the party were usually sorted out by the 8th Section, which rarely had recourse to the security police.) In 1967 Novotný tried to intimidate restless intellectuals, by permitting the security police to stage another public trial of the writer Beneš and of several students for subversion and espionage. To save his own position, in December 1967, Novotný was alleged to have ordered the 8th Section's chief, Mamula, to prepare lists of factional opponents to be arrested. But, by then, the very security agents refused to move, because they probably came to realize that they would be blamed and suffer for whatever they uncovered.

After Novotný's fall in 1968, the security (political) police was finally dismantled and largely dissolved. Curiously enough, the Minister of the Interior still contained a "small" section headed by Lieutenant Colonel Šalgovič, Deputy Minister, whose task it was to function as a counter-espionage service. For this purpose the section also retained two Soviet security advisors, Nazorov and Byeloturkin, who were only expelled from the service and the country, when the

Soviet armies moved to occcupy Czechoslovakia in August 1968. Soviet advisors had been in Czechoslovakia since 1949; Barák also had an advisor (Nedvedev), so had his successors Štrougal and Kudrna, but Nazarov and Byeloturkin proved particularly obnoxious: they prepared security measures for the invading armies.

CONCLUSIONS

Can a country with a democratic tradition be transformed into a totalitarian party-state? Judging from the Czechoslovak experience it is possible, but with certain qualifications. There are limits to the efficacity of the system which cannot be transgressed in such a country. As, for example, the fact that Czech and Slovak communists proved incapable of installing their own totalitarian terror, with all that it involved, show trials, torture as means of investigation, mass executions and burials of victims in mass graves, etc. This had to be done on their behalf by experienced Soviet allies. Terror, however, impressed party members only; the population as such was unimpressed and continued its own separate existence outside party influence and control. If terror structures existed in Czechoslovakia, its operators used them only reluctantly, as the last days of communism in the country prove conclusively: to apply violence efficiently the Czechoslovak services required Soviet orders! Thus, the repression of the November 1989 demonstration was ordered by the KGB advisors and had unforeseen consequences.

Otherwise Czechoslovak totalitarian structures proved as vulnerable as the democratic ones, if faced with a determined resistance of the population. In 1948, the communist party mobilised for its coup d'Etat in Prague a large section of the population. The democratic system resisted for three weeks, but then suddenly collapsed. In 1989, ten days were sufficient for communist totalitarianism to collapse, faced with a mobilisation of the entire population in Prague and subsequently of the whole country.

However, if Czechoslovak communism could keep power with terror, its dependence on the Soviet system was total. As it was seen, the regime could not make use of terrorism without Soviet advice. Since its very existence was linked with the Soviet system, its obedience was abject. If we take the year 1968 as an example of disobedience, this argument becomes self-evident. It is true that Husák resisted Gorbachev's pressure to start perestroyka and glasnost in Czechoslovakia, but ultimately he had to give in, as Czechoslovak communism could not survive without Soviet guiding help. In other words Soviet communists installed communism in Czechslovakia, but also 'liquidated' it.

If, in 1948, the communist coup d'Etat was successful because of wartime demoralization, in 1968, Soviet armies had to restore obedience and communism in the country. By then, the entire population realised the incredible stagnation that Czechoslovakia, once a prosperous little country, found itself in, because of communism. But, because of the Soviet communist party's power, it had to go on enduring it, perhaps for ever. As soon as the population of Czechoslovakia became convinced that Gorbachev's perestroyka changed fundamentally this basic dependence and obedience of Czechoslovak communism to Soviet totalitarianism, it simply rebelled and abolished it. Communism ended ignominiously after some 42 years, leaving the country devastated materially and spiritually. It can now serve as a case study of historical political systems and a warning to all free people, even to those living in utter misery. The system solved none of the world's problems, and it left behind hecatombes of human victims, 60 million in the USSR alone.

BIBLIOGRAPHICAL REMARKS

There is a lack of general histories of this period. Czech and Slovak historians found it politically risky to write about it as individuals. They, therefore, hide behind collective works such as Přehled československých dějin (Survey of Czechoslovak History), vol. 3, Prague 1955 or Dějiny KSČ (History of the Communist Party of Czechoslovakia), Prague, 1961; moreover these works are based on ideological premises and are unreadable. I wrote my own introduction in 1971 Czechoslovakia: A Short History (Edinburgh University Press) and W. V. Wallace a more academic introduction, Czechoslovakia: Modern History, in 1974. With politics in Czechoslovakia it is even worse. There is no political science treatment in Czech or Slovak. In English there is Professor Taborský's Communism in Czechoslovakia, 1948–60, (Princeton 1961); Professor Ulč's Politics in Czechoslovakia (San Francisco, 1970); and my own Politics in Czechoslovakia, 1945–1971 (Washington 1981). The following books and documents were consulted: R. Luža, The Transfer of Sudeten Germans (London 1964); J. Král, Otázky hospodářsko a socialního vývoje v českých zemích (Questions of Economic and Social Development in the Czech Provinces) (Prague 1957 vol. 3); J. Kalvoda, Czechoslovakia's Role in Soviet Strategy (Washington 1978); J. Matoušek, Slovenské národné orgány (Slovak National Administration), (Bratislava 1960); F. Němec, V. Moudrý, The Soviet Seizure of Transcarpathian Ruthenia (Toronto 1955); Brno v minulosti (Brno in the Past) (Brno 1960); K. Bartošek, Pražské povstání 1945 (The Prague Uprising in 1945) (Prague 1965); British Foreign Office documents: 371/56085/1945; WO/193/303/1945; 371/47124/1945.

On the pre-Communist period the following books and documents are particularly valuable: J. Opat, O novou demokracii (About A New Demcoracy) (Prague 1966); J. Hendrych, A. Šrámek, Československá státní správa (Czechoslovak State Administration) (Prague 1973); B. Bunža, Le parti populaire tchácoslovaque (Rome 1971); J. Horák, The

Czechoslovak Social Democratic Party 1938–1945 (Columbia University 1960); Revue dějin socialismu (Historical Review of Socialism) no. 8/1968; Příspěvky k dějinám KSČ (Contributions to CPCz History) no. 5/1963, no. 6/1962, no. 4/1963, no. 4/1962; Otázky nárondní a demodratické revoluce v ČSR (Question of National and Democratic Revolution in Czechoslovakia) (Prague 1955; FO 181/933/1945; 371/ 56081/1946; 817/1946. J. Bradley, Le systéme et la vie politique en Tchécoslovaquie de 1945 au coup de Prague en 1948, Canadian Journal of Political Science XV/3/1982; Dějiny KSČ (A History of the CzCP) (Prague 1961). Únor 1948 Sborník dokumentů (February 1948. Selected Documents) (Prague 1958); Dějiny a součastnost (Contemporary History) no. 7/1968; J. Veselý, Kronika únorových dnů 1948 (A Chronicle of February 1948 Days) (Prague 1959); M. Bouček, M. Klimeš, Dramatické dny února 1948 (The Dramatic Days of February 1948) (Prague 1973); J. Kobel, The Communist Subversion in Czechoslovakia (London 1959); P. E. Zinner, Communist Strategy and Tactics in Czechoslovakia (London 1963); Historica, no. 5/1963; FO 371/65787/1947; 371/ 71329/1947; 371/772468/1948; Top Secret US OSS/ 19.6.1948; Top Secret US CX/13.12.1947. K. Kaplan, Utváření generální linie výstavby socialismu v Československu (The Formation of a General Line for Building of Socialism is Czechoslovakia), (Prague 1966); Sborník historický (Prague 12/1964); Československý časopis historický (Czechoslovak History Journal) (Prague 1973/5).

On the Communist period the following books and documents are particularly valuable: Revue dějin socialismu (Historical Review of Socialism) (Prague 1969/4); Historie a vojenství (History and Military Science) (Prague 1973/1,2; A. Neuman, Nový právní řád v lidové demokracii (A New Legal System in People's Democracy) (Prague 1952); Dějiny a součastnost (Contemporary History) (Prague 1968/ 8); Dějiny university v Brně (History of Brno University) (Brno 1969). J. Dolanský, Tři léta plánovaní v lidové demokratickém Československu (Three Years of Planning in People's Democratic Czechoslovakia) (Prague 1949); Příspěvky k dějinám KSČ (Contributions to CzCP History) (Prague 1963/5; 1967/6. J. Opat, o novou demokracii (On New Democracy) (Prague 1966); Příspěvky k kějinam KSČ 1962/12/ 1967/1; Dějiny a součastnost (Prague 1968/8); (The Czechoslovak Political Trials, 1950–1954 (London 1971). J. Bradley, Prague Spring 1968 In Historical Perspective, (Eastern European Quarterly XVI/3/ 1982); Revue dějin socialismu (Prague 1969/2); Život strany (Party Life) (Prague 1968/7); G. Golan, The Czechoslovak Reform Movement (Cambridge 1971): P. Tigrid, Le Printemps de Prague (Paris 1968); Sedm pražských dnů (Seven Days in Prague) (Prague 1968); Tanky proti sjezdu (Tanks against the Congress) (Vienna 1970). H. Gordon Skilling, Czechoslovakia's Interrupted Revolution (Princeton 1976); Československá federace (Czechoslovak Federation) (Prague 1969– 4 vols); V. Mastný, Czechoslovakia: Crisis in World Communism, (New York 1972); on Husák's fall see the daily information bulletins of the Civic Forum 1989.